יוֹם כִּפּוּר
as Manifest in an Approaching Dorsal Fin

Adam Byrn Tritt

SMITHCRAFT
PRESS

Copyright © 2013 by Adam Byrn Tritt. All rights reserved. This book or any portion thereof may not be reproduced or used in any manner whatsoever without the express written permission of the publisher except for the use of brief quotations in a book review.

ISBN 978-1-62927-001-2

Smithcraft Press
1921 Michels Drive NE
Palm Bay, FL 32905

www.SmithcraftPress.com

Yom Kippur as Manifest in an Approaching Dorsal Fin

Contents

Dedication vii

Yom Kippur as Manifest in
   an Approaching Dorsal Fin 1

3:10 27

Funeral, Expurgated 29

Passover and the
   Industrial Revolution 79

The Harmony of Broken Glass 87

Fifty Years 107

Yahrzeit 109

What Do Jews Do on Christmas? . . 141

About the Author 145

To my ancestors

and to my family,
especially the ones who
no longer talk to me,
because it is from them that
I have learned the most.

Yom Kippur as Manifest in an Approaching Dorsal Fin

It is Yom Kippur. A Monday. I have taken the day off work to walk, meditate, think. I have taken the day off work so I could go to temple the night before and not worry about the time, the hour, how late it was getting, when I would need to get up.

We asked our friends to go with us. In our back yard, playing with clay, our conversation set on cognates and religion. I mentioned the Buddha of compassion, Amitabha, and the other name for him, Amida. How the Amidah is the name of a prayer of compassion during Yom Kippur. How it relates to the fruit, almonds, as the ancient Hebrews saw the almond as a symbol for watchfulness, promises, and redemption. How the part of the brain which we know to be the seat of our ability to see things in a global, compassionate way is called the amygdala, from the Greek *amugdalē*, meaning almond. Craig started talking about the Kol Nidre prayer and, being Craig, translated it for us and we sat, transfixed, as often we do listening to Craig. Lee, Evanne, Beth, and I, listening to Craig.

Of course we listen to Craig. He, translator of dead languages. He, who juggles biblical text back and forth from language to language, from meaning to meaning as if the passages are but palm-sized bean bags. He, of three books of translations. Yes, we listen when he speaks.

As we talked, we discovered he had never been to temple, had never actually listened to the Kol Nidre. Neither had Beth, nor Evanne—and that, of course, was not a surprise, growing up in the Midwest: Ohio and Nebraska, Methodist. Right then, we asked if they'd like to go with us this Yom Kippur, to the Kol Nidre service: the only one we go to.

They were surprised. Craig said he was honored. Evanne agreed with a clear look of shock on her face. Beth asked if we're sure it was OK and told us how special it was to be asked, how appreciated it was.

That was months ago. We asked the small, local temple if we could come and bring three guests. No problem. May we have their names, and do they have any departed they would like Yizkor candles for? Yes. We were set to go.

Erev Yom Kippur arrives. Lee is under the weather and cannot go. She asks that I go anyway and I resist but she does not want to disappoint our friends.

Evanne worries whether she should have her hair covered. Beth is concerned she looks like "a goy." Lee tells her, jokingly, that she should proudly announce she is a shiksa. I suggest against it and let them know it is an honor that they are going and the congregation would be overjoyed they are there.

They are worried. No need to dress well, not for this congregation. But they do, and

Beth's high heels put her so high above me she has to bend over and I must tip myself up on my toes to kiss her on the cheek.

Both wear black, notice their shoes are made of leather, and point out they have worn black once they discover the color of the holy day is white. No one will be following all these rules. No one will notice.

Evanne, married, wears a scarf on her head, long and flowing, tied into her hair, nearly as long, nearly to her thighs. She could be Golda and Tevye's shorter, forgotten daughter. She could be from the shtetle. No one will guess she isn't Jewish. Beth actually looks Jewish and no one tells her this. How to explain what that looks like?

Craig fits in perfectly but is wearing shoes for the first time in, perhaps, more than a year. I offer him one of my tallit (prayer shawls) and a kipa I think will fit him well, gold and silver. He tells me again he is honored to be invited and I am privileged to give him my tallis to wear.

We arrive, are greeted, take prayer books, and I search for a large print version, find one, enter, find a place in the pews close to the front. Myself, Evanne, Beth, and Craig. I leave space to my right, where Lee would sit, where I would be able to see her.

We talk, discuss translation, Craig notices the Kol Nidre in the prayer book is not translated literally and, a game of telephone, shows me the text clues by showing Beth who shows Evanne who shows me, differences in font, serif versus sans serif, that tell a careful reader what is a translation and what is a paraphrase.

This congregation, Mateh Chaim, has as yet no home. And yet we have been welcomed even though we swell their ranks and the available room. Even though there are non-Jews among us who need not be here. The congregation is growing and hopes to have a home, but there is, in thoughtful congregations, a balance between the need for a building and the needs of community: the understanding that an edifice takes money which many of the people here tonight don't have. It is the only congregation in Palm Bay. It meets tonight in a Methodist church. Behind the portable ark, containing the Torah, is a twenty-foot cross. It is not the building that makes a congregation.

I do not mind this so much. We talk, quietly, as we would before any service. Evanne tells us she is glad to see me misbehaving as usual as it puts her at ease.

"Misbehaving?" I ask. She answers I have said "ass" twice since sitting down in the pews. She says it like this: "You said a-$-$ twice since sitting your a-$-$ down." Silly. Anglo Saxon not allowed for a Methodist?

I think, momentarily, of our Yom Kippur in North Carolina. We were alone. No one around us had an understanding. I listened to Kol Nidre on Internet radio.

Joel Fleishman had a similar experience on the television program *Northern Exposure* in an episode called "Shofar, So Good" (1994) when, on Yom Kippur, he was visited by Rabbi Schulman. Our program opens with Joel, physician to Cicely, Alaska, carbo-loading in preparation for his day of fasting. He is attempting to explain Yom Kippur to the ever-interested residents as they eat at the Brick, the inn and tavern, and has little success. This is mostly because he has only a tenuous, superficial understanding himself. He knows the words, he knows the rules and proscriptions, takes care to keep the fast, not wash, not to care for personal convenience, to give the day up to feeling keenly, sharply one's place in the world and relationship to God and our fellows. He sees the holiday as a noun with a set of rules, not a verb with a set of tools. To Joel, it is no longer a living tradition, and he does not know what to do with it. On top of this, he is lonely for those who know his tradition.

Our Good Doctor Joel, while in the midst of his fast, was visited by the Good Rabbi Schulman who, as surprised as Joel, was lifted by a shaft of light and deposited in Cicely to help Joel understand what Yom Kippur is really about, and Dr. Fleishman begins the process of making amends. It is a journey, a Hebrew Dickensian vision quest, which starts with the Good Rabbi occupying the space of the top head of a totem pole. Jews, after all, are tribal too.

Not too surprisingly, the characters on the show who understand Yom Kippur best are the shamans.

But I am not alone and I revel in this. Craig tells us the history of the Kol Nidre. The actual translation, the "Kol Nidre controversy" surrounding just what the proper place and ramification of the prayer is.

Kol nidre means "all vows," and it absolves us of vows and promises made that we needed to make to survive but knew were wrong. It apologizes and gives release from the many times we said Yes when we wanted to say No, but did not because our jobs, food on the table, roofs over our heads, our safety, our security meant we had to say one thing, do one thing, when another was what we knew was proper.

He explains, my teaching middle school is my Kol Nidre. My giving grades, requiring students to do what they have no desire to, that is my Kol Nidre. When I teach them to pass a test when they want to learn creativity, that is my Kol Nidre. When I do that which I must to put bring food and security, when I do not call those around me on their actions because I must protect my job, that is my Kol Nidre. When I do not, can not, must not act in accordance with my true self:

Yom Kippur as Manifest . . .

my Kol Nidre. When I do something I must instead of write and create. Kol Nidre.

Evanne points out that is exactly what the abbot at the Thai Buddhist temple told me, that I was doing what I needed to and need only recognize that and the needs of fitting into our community and of survival and taken into account in the realm of Karma.

Yet even those vows I take seriously. I uttered them. And so the Kol Nidre also protects us from ourselves; we make this prayer because we take vows so seriously that we consider ourselves bound even if we make them under duress or in times of stress when we are not thinking straight.

The Rabbi, Fred Natkin, walks up to the bima (stage) and we look around. No fashion show here. Women in pants, men in dungarees, vests. Hats instead of kipas. I have done this as well as it is more comfortable, does not fall off, shades my eyes when reading. Many women have Tallit and that is a sure sign of a rather liberal welcoming congregation.

The service starts and it is with great participation of the congregation, coming up to the bima, sitting down again after hugs and kisses. Always each moment, each prayer ends with hugs and kisses among all those on the bima. Evanne asks me if this is important. Among many liberal congregations, this is common, important, this contact and affection. I say it is a fitting way to end a prayer to love each other and who are we to argue, and I lean over and kiss Evanne on the cheek.

The congregation prays, meditates, responds; the rabbi sings, chants.

The time has come for the sermon. The rabbi speaks of science fiction. Reads a letter written by him to the neighboring Moslem congregation offering aid and friendship after a shooting into the mosque this week. He is offering for the descendants of the two sons of Abraham, the children of Isaac and the children of Ishmael, to make peace and fight together for justice. The Jewish high holy days and Ramadan started the same day. We have the same goals. The president of the congregation writes his thanks, appreciation, and friendship in a letter to the newspaper, thanking the rabbi and congregation. He reminds us we must make the world the heaven we wish it to be. It is our job and what we are chosen to do. That we do not pray for peace, but pray to *be* peace. That Judaism is a religion of verbs. The prayers re-commence.

The Kol Nidre is sung. There are two tunes for this prayer. I was taught by a rabbi there is magic in the tunes themselves, in the music, so, if one does not know the words, hum, dai de dai, la la la, and that is good and will do the trick. But I want to sing and this is the other tune, the one Lee knows. It is the Sephardic tune, I believe, the one from the Middle East and not the Ashkenazic tune of Eastern Europe and Eurasia. I do my best. Craig knows the words but does not sing, unfamiliar with the tune even more than I. Evanne, somehow, reads more loudly than others, seems to fit, sounds clear, and I am frequently amazed by this.

More prayers, meditations, the Amidah and call for compassion. I feel this prayer as I did the Kol Nidre and look for my wife, see the empty space. I think of my own Yom Kippur prayer. And when I have trouble following along, I recite it to myself:

We open our mouths to proclaim how beautiful the world is, how sweet life is and how dear to us you are, Lady, Mother of All Living.

We stand here today to remind ourselves that we are all part of this web of creation. We are all linked, so that what any of us do affects all of us, and that we are all responsible for the Earth, and each other. We have chosen to be here today as a symbol of our commitment, our awareness of this connection.

Even so, we forget our promises and our duties.

We gossip, we mock, we jeer.

We quarrel, we are unkind, we lie.

We neglect, we abuse, we betray.

We are cruel, we hate, we destroy.

We are careless, we are violent, we steal.

We are jealous, we oppress, we are xenophobic.

We are racist, we are sexist, we are homophobic.

We waste, we pollute, we are selfish.

Yom Kippur as Manifest . . .

> We disregard the sufferings of others, we allow others to suffer for our ignorance and our pride.
> We hurt each other willingly and unwillingly.
> We betray each other with violence and with stealth.
> And most of all, we resist the impulse to do what we know is good, and we do not resist the impulse to do what we know is bad.
> All this we acknowledge to be true, and we do not blame the mirror if the reflection displeases.
> Lady, help us to forgive each other for all we have done and help us to do better in the coming year. Bring us into harmony with the Earth and all Her ways.
> So mote it be!

In this prayer, we admit we are not perfect and proclaim we will make good on our mistakes even if we are not aware we have made them. We all make such mistakes. Such is the friction, the *dukkuh* as the Tibetans call it, of life. And we must have the compassion for others to apologize, to make amends, person to person. If we do not, we cannot go into the new year. If they do not accept, the guilt is on their heads if, and only truly if, we have honestly done our best to make amends.

We must also have compassion for ourselves and the ways we have transgressed against ourselves. Such is the message of the Amidah and Kol Nidre; we can start over and do better. Such is the message from Amida, Amitabha.

And we are cognizant we have made mistakes we are unaware of individually. For these, we say a prayer and ask forgiveness not of God, but of each other and offer our forgiveness as well.

More meditations, kisses, hugs. Then the Mourner's Kaddish, and I quietly remind those with me this is what they gave those the names of the departed for. I think of those I have lost and feel keenly the empty space next to me, where my wife should be, and move slightly over more, closer to Evanne, leaving more room for my absent wife as though I was looking to be able to see her as I sang, but could not find her. I am missing her and think, sadly, at some point this space will be open, open and empty and not fillable. Thus says this prayer.

And with this, service ends. Craig mentions how so many of these prayers have been taken, nearly without change, for Christian services. Beth feels the continuity with the Methodist services with which she is familiar. We exit, putting our books back as we do, and head back to the house.

Lee greets us outside, still not feeling well but wanting to be social to a degree. I am grateful, and tell my friends so, that I was able to go to temple with those I love even when my own dear was at home. I was able to share this evening with them, this prayer, this holy day. I am grateful to them and happy.

They had said it was an honor to be asked. That night they repeated their gratitude and surprise. It is I who am grateful. It is I who am honored. It is I who am, again, surprised, amazed, and smiling. I hold them both and say thank you, then smile as they drive away.

Today I stay home for Yom Kippur. I do not go to temple, however. I plan to write, run, walk, meditate, remain quiet.

I get ready to go to the beach. On days like this I am reminded of some of the perks to living in Florida. It is October and I am going for a run on the beach. My ancestors would already be cold, wearing thick coats and having long collected the winter wood. I will be running by the waves wearing as little as I can get away with. I say to Lee, listening, that it is too hot to wear dungaree shorts, the only kind I have. I have two swimsuits, both old, hardly worn but seeming worn, nonetheless, elastics given up their ability to stretch, become brittle.

I have not purchased any in years and told myself I would not until my weight was down to where I wanted it. I might have to go back and revisit that idea. They were too small for years and I would not go to the beach. Now they are too big and are unfit, do not fit, I put on the one with the best elastic. My wife shakes her head. No? Why not? Does it have a lining? No. She tells me I have lost weight and that will lead to needing a lining if I am

Yom Kippur as Manifest...

planning on going running. She does not want me to be uncomfortable or, worse, injure myself, telling me the fat I used to have kept some things in place and, without that weight, I'll want that lining as I go jangling up and down. I put on the other suit and it falls off. It has a cord, I pull it tight. It still hangs a bit and I'll need a new suit soon.

I go off to Melbourne Beach and leave everything, including my sandals, in the car. Keys, wallet, glasses. I put about fifty cents in the meter and get one hour and fifteen minutes for my coins. I did not take sunscreen so I leave my shirt on, planning to take it off if I get too hot.

It is bright, clear, brilliant and the beach is quiet and nearly empty. I head to the shoreline and walk, briskly, south.

I practice an exercise as I go called the Walk for Atonement. At-one-ment, removing separation. Becoming one with what is around me, with the world and all that is in it. With time and space. If we felt at one with all things, who would we, who could we, hurt?

What is our place in this world? What is our place, in context to all that is? I walk.

With my steps, I contemplate spans of time. A day. What does a day feel like? What does it feel like to exist a day? A year. How does a year feel? Ten years. Can I feel ten years? How plastic I am. How much one can change in ten years.

I do this every year. From then to one hundred. This year, I add fifty years. Fifty years. I am approaching that and can feel it. It is not far beyond my span now and I can understand that in a personal context. One hundred years. What does that feel like? I have and had relatives nearly that old. One thousand years. I can understand this historically but what does it feel like? I am uncertain. My place in it is, or can be, nearly a tenth. But how much a part do I actually play? My grasp on it is tenuous. Ten thousand years. Again, historically, I have an idea. Personally, it is too vast, too long. I have no context. What is my place in that span of time? Nearly none. One hundred thousand? None. None at all. A million?

As I reach a million, I see something I have never seen but which is astonishingly familiar in the water a scant twenty feet from me:

Yom Kippur as Manifest . . .

a triangular dorsal fin, a triangular tail fin, both moving gracefully in the water so close if I wanted to, if I were fool enough, I could walk out to it and barely have my calves half-covered by ocean. This is amazingly close for a shark.

I stand and watch. This is an interruption in the flow of the meditation. Or is it? A shark comes so close as I contemplate a million years and this seems like a message. It feels like a hello from distance of time and I can see, now, what that million years looks like. I cannot go to it so it, instead, has come to me. Today.

I am aware of a person next to me, fewer than a few feet away. "Is that what I think it is?"

What else could he be asking? It is safe, I imagine, to answer in the affirmative. "Yes."

"I was going to go swimming."

"Still going to?"

"I just moved here. This is my first time at the beach. Are they out there all the time?"

"Are you asking me if there are always sharks out there, or if death is always fewer than twenty feet away and swimming around us?"

He stares at me.

"The answer is yes to both," I tell him. "You're just getting to see it today. Welcome to Florida. If you plan on hiking instead, remember, we're the only state with all four kinds of venomous snakes."

He walks off.

I continue my walk. With each step I think of a person I have wronged. I apologize. With the next step, I forgive myself as well. I do this until I can think of no more people, but I am human and I must have hurt more people than I think simply by the act of living. I apologize, with each step, contemplating the many ways we hurt each other and never know it, cannot help it. And, when this is done, forgive myself.

As I continue to walk, I think of each person I know has hurt me. I forgive them. It no longer matters. In the span of time, what could it matter? If they have not admitted guilt, what does it matter? I forgive them. I forgive them all. If I have thought badly of them for the wrong they have done, for this, even, I apologize and forgive myself.

Why carry guilt? Why carry anger? Why carry a careless word? Of what use is it in the span of years? A million years, and how long am I here? There is a shark in the water.

Ga-te, ga-te, Pāra-ga-te, Pāra-sam-ga-te, Bodhi svā-hā. Gone, gone. Beyond gone. Past beyond gone. There is enlightenment.

I start to run. Barefoot I pad the sand beneath me. Step by step following the mean line of the surf. If the waves come in further, I lift my legs higher, pull up my knees, splash as each sole descends. This varies my running, changes the muscles used, increases my activity.

With each footfall, I think of a year of my life. A year. Each time I pad the sand beneath me; grains millions of years in creation, millions in erosion. Each step, a year. I run out of years quickly, in a matter of half a minute. I think of my potential lifespan and run them out in another half minute.

I think then of the people I love and run them out, each step a year of life. My family, less than a minute each, like the blink in time they are, we are. My friends, a minute. I think of those I know, enjoy the company of, gone in minutes, and I do this consecutively but I know it is all concurrent, all gone, more or less, in the steps it takes me to run out mine. I think of those I don't like. All gone too. No different. All the same. We are a set of footprints. We wash away.

I wish all people happiness and the root of happiness. I wish all people freedom from suffering and the root of suffering. Even those I don't like. Especially. Now, before I become invisible among the sands. Now, before I wash away.

I have run out of people. I have not run out of beach. I continue, watching the sandpipers skitter the foamline as I splash and make impressions which are instantly gone behind me as the tide washes out. I run and am not tired. How much further?

I expected to run for a few minutes. I thought, how long can I run before I need to turn back? How far can I go before I know I am half-spent and turn around to run back or all spent and must walk my way back? But neither point comes. I run.

Yom Kippur as Manifest . . .

I run easily, no pain, barely sweating, my heart slow, my breathing calm. It was not long ago I would run five minutes and be exhausted. I would run and walk and run and walk in alternate minutes. Now I am easy and feel free and comfortable, open. How long have I been running?

I choose a point in the distance, a home among the many but different in color than most, and decide to run to that, then turn around. On the return I can sense no reason to be heading back but my desire to return to my writing. Still, I am not tired, not worn, my breathing slow and full.

I see the salmon-hued building that signals where I started. There is the boardwalk, invisible behind the sea oats and dunes. I run up to the ramp and there I stop.

Once to my car, I look at the meter. I have been gone more than an hour and a quarter and it flashes at me. I have run for much of that time. I have run for nearly an hour. It is not a marathon, but it is an amazement, an accomplishment, and I have a sudden keen sense I have not eaten anything today but half a cup of milk. I am not fasting. I cannot fast.

It is bad for my health and is, therefore, forbidden by Talmudic law. Certain people and people under certain conditions, according to the Talmud, may not fast. I have brought nothing by way of food with me and across the empty street is a Coldstone.

I get my things from the car, brush off my feet, put my sandals on, put another quarter into the meter and walk over. What could make this day more perfect than adding an ice cream?

There is a Starbucks, on one side of it and, on the other, a Bizarro's Pizza. There used to be café here Lee and I ate at once; had lunch with Jeannie, Joseph, and Connor on our first visit to Melbourne. It left with Frances, or Wilma, or one of the September storms to visit in 2004. The building is still empty, partial.

I walk into Coldstone. It is slightly after twelve and it feels as though there have been few customers today. I ask the young lady behind the counter for plain ice cream with no fat and no sugar. They have ice cream with no flavoring; simply the taste of milk, crystalized, thick and solid. No sweetener. Why would milk need sugar? She is happy to oblige and what size? One cup. A small.

Would you like anything in that? No. Wait, yes.

Please, if you would, some almonds.

3:10

It is 3:10 AM
And I'm
Wrestling with Hashem
Over matters of love
And propriety,
Over poetry
And the small matter
Of whether he exists.
Hashem states
It is if little consequence
And I say, Hashem,
People fight and die,
Live, love, kill and
Become kind
In your name
And Hashem argues
Atheists do the same
But are, at least,
Honest in their motives.

Funeral, Expurgated

My wife tells me she cannot believe what writers have to do. They must bare their souls, score their psyches raw and place what is inside, outside, on paper, in an artistic manner. And we must make it sound as though it was effortless and fun.

True enough. That's the fun part. I think every writer is an exhibitionist to some degree and, perhaps, a bit of a masochist. Or martyr. Or minister. The act of writing, for me, must be sacred.

It also takes bravery to be a writer. This observation comes not from me but, again, from my esteemed helpmate, my goddess incarnate, she who is the Joy of the Universe and Queen of Creation: my wife.

She states she cannot imagine the difficulty of having scraped the emotion from the soul and then putting it out in public where the people will not only read of our own exterior and interior lives but those of others as well and then judge how artfully or entertainingly we have rendered them. How do we not hurt feelings, bruise hearts, hide that cause which is private while making public the effects? How do writers not end up either ineffective, with a social network intact, or effective and read but friendless and lonely? How do we not alienate our families and friends?

Who says we don't?

I have struggled with this. How much to say? What to leave out? How does an essayist balance narrative with personal relationships? I have no idea but know I will struggle with this again and again in essay after essay. I expose what I need but leave out what does not move the concept forward, support the idea, make more clear the conceit and reality I wish the reader to experience.

But my idea of what needs to be exposed and what does not may be fully different than that of the person suffering the exposure. As

Funeral, Expurgated

a family member or friend is feeling left naked in the wind while I am thinking I did nothing more than describe his hat.

I am going to be brave now. It's all I know to do. I'm sorry.

When I die I want to be dropped off a cliff.

Or left in a forest. That would be fine as well. Throw a party. Say what you will. Cry, laugh. Recall anything I might have done of worth. Remember anything I might have done or said that made you smile. Please forget any act or utterance of mine which might have caused hurt or pain as you'll know it was not done of meanness or cruelty, but of the ignorance we all share as the fallible humans we are.

Make no marker. If my deeds are of worth, people will remember them. And the hunt to find my grave or remains may prove quite a cottage industry. On the other hand, if I have left nothing of worth no one will look for me. If I am not memorable, no marker will make me so.

It is Thursday night. The phone rings twice. Lee, my wife, answers it. It is late, nearly ten-thirty at night, and seldom does the house phone ring at any time but still less at this hour. Anyone we want to talk with has our cell numbers. Those phones are off now and this call is either a wrong number or important.

"It was your father. It sounds serious. He wants you to call him." I do.

"I wanted you to know your grandmother is in the hospital. She is catatonic and the funeral will be anywhere from two days from now to two weeks. I'd like for you to be there."

I expect to hear more of her condition but he talks only of the funeral. I will be there and tell him so. I will go for him. There is no other reason.

A day passes and I look at my calendar, mark all the days a funeral would be an inconvenience in the next two weeks. There is statewide testing at our school on Monday and Tuesday, and then two days of the same the week after. A writing conference the next weekend. I will miss what I miss but would rather not. I'd rather not go at all.

Funeral, Expurgated

Monday comes and I ask about the bereavement policy of our school board. There is none. One takes sick leave. I fill out the forms in advance and leave them with the secretary. She gives me her home number in case I find, in the night or early morning, the need to drive south to Delray instead of to work or, when away, if I need to let them know I need extra days. Candy asks if I don't want to leave now, to be there when my grandmother dies. No. That is not necessary. I don't explain. She is kind, soft, and I would guess knew her grandmother well.

Wednesday morning. Early, and I am at school, as usual, by eight-fifteen. Monday was the first day of statewide testing. All day. Tuesday was the second. The next day for testing is the Monday to follow and finally I have the chance to teach. I have planned to introduce the concepts of archetypes and archetypal themes, characters, and symbols, and have the students search these out in a film before delving into written literature. I am teaching the first of five classes today and have barely finished one day of a four-day lesson when my phone rings.

My wife has called, the front office secretary tells me, and it is important I call her back. Lee never calls me at work. I know what this is and, excusing myself to my students, call her. My grandmother died at eight-fifteen that morning.

I pause, wait, nothing. I expected not to feel much but nothing was much less than anticipated. There just wasn't anything there. I say thank you, tell her I'm going to go to the office and let them know I need to leave as soon as is practical. I tell her I love her and put down the phone. My students are listening. The bell for second period rings and I leave the room, as the students do, to find the assistant principal.

Arrangements are quickly made and the AP, a kind, helpful soul, follows me back to my class where students are waiting outside my door. They know something must be up. We enter, I gather my things while I hurriedly discuss with Mr. Kaminski how to explain the lesson, written on the board, to the sub. I know I will have to redo this. He tells me not to worry and I grab my things and leave.

Funeral, Expurgated

Off to my son's high school five minutes away. I check him out and we head home to pack. We have no funeral clothes. What we have will do. Black dungarees, a black shirt and shoes for me, the same for Alek. All into bags. Bags into the truck. Truck onto the road south. It is barely edging toward eleven in the morning.

We drive. Alek asks me for no stories of her. He knows there are few to hear and he has heard them all. He has met her on a few occasions, his great-grandmother, but she knew little about him. She would talk to us continuously of her other grandchildren, the wonders they had produced and challenges over which they had prevailed. Alek would listen, politely. Always politely, quietly. She once offered him ten dollars to talk. What did he have to say? That is his memory of her. He is her second great-grandchild.

When my daughter was born, in 1985, my grandmother grilled my wife. There is no other word for it. It was the type of questioning often reserved for congressional hearings or associated with cop movies where the suspect sits, uncomfortable, in an interrogation room, under a bright bare bulb. What did she need, how much are such things? How hard was I working and why didn't we have enough? In the end, she sent my grandfather out to the car to get the checkbook, wrote for a moment, enclosed it in a card, put it into an envelope and sealed, it handing it immediately to Lee. It was one hundred dollars. The total Sef received over time, given in one lump sum. All she'd ever give for her first great-grandchild.

My father would insist I visit, and we did. He would ask me to call and always I did, whether asked or not. The conversations were short, brusque. I would ask questions and she might answer or not. She would ask how we all were and the response to all my answers were either "That's nice" for things that had gone well or "Well, what can you expect?" for anything that had not. As the years passed I learned never to mention anything that was not perfect and the conversations became deep with lies and façades.

"Call," my father would say, and then would tell me all about the land and buildings, the factory owned by my grandmother. He would

Funeral, Expurgated

explain of the inheritance and how much I could expect. That is one of my earliest memories involving her, in truth: his talk of inheritance and wills and the wrangling among him, his elder sister, and younger brother.

I expected no inheritance. I never did. But I called and visited anyway because it was right to do so. I brought the children against their protests to sit in the uncomfortable, hard chairs, avoid the expensive antiques.

I do have some earlier memories of her and my grandfather. Some. I think of these as we drive to Delray on 95 and then the turnpike. The long childhood drive from New Jersey. Perth Amboy or Somerset. Interminable to a four-year-old, a five-year-old. Up to Rockland County, New York. To a large house on a hill. Steep, shallow slate steps up to a door on a wide porch. A kitchen door that swung either way. A closet with a door in the back and, behind that door, steep steps of stone through a narrow wood stairwell leading up to the attic and books. I sat up there, thinking I was in a secret place. It smelled of mold from the wooden walls, from the slate steps, the books. Moist and dank like a cave. Dark and quiet above the house, feeling I was beneath it all. Today, I recognize that scent, that specific smell of mold from old books and wood. I smell it in caves. It is a comfort I cannot express and I don't understand coming from the deepest part of the human brain, deep from the limbic system; the scent is warm and comfortable. My fondest memory of my grandmother is the smell of mold.

It was in this house, my mother told me again and again, that she was offered ten thousand dollars to stop dating my father. Perhaps she should have taken it. It was in this house that my aunt, my father's older sister, accused my mother of wanting nothing from them but money. A strange accusation considering she could have taken the ten thousand and still dated my father but did not. My mother responded by slapping her.

That is all I know of that house.

My grandmother came from Austria. That is nearly all I know of my grandmother. She had money. She owned a furniture factory, and she came from Austria.

At some point they moved to Israel. Then they moved to Delray, Florida, into a condo.

Funeral, Expurgated

My father would go up often on errands of a surreptitious nature. Anytime my grandfather wanted to buy something, he would have to ferret the money away and slip it to my father. Then my father would buy it and bring it over as a gift. A computer. A boombox. All were "gifts" from my father.

If I were out with my father, regardless of the reason or destination, I would have to be quiet if my grandparents called on the cell phone. I do not know why this is. My father would mouth silent words. I cannot see well enough to read lips. He would not repeat what he said, ever, in any audible form, so still I have no idea what he was telling me.

If we, my father and I, my parents and I, all of us and my children—regardless of the combination—if my father was there and we were going out to dinner, to a store, and his parents called, he would lie about our location or destination. He would tell me later his mother was never to know we spent money. How did she think my father's house was furnished? Where did she think the multiple matching computers or identical matching half-dozen cell phones and the latest of whatever gadget was hot came from? She could not know money was spent and any money spent was a secret. Things purchased for my grandfather became tangible constant lies. Their condo was full of them. Nothing was his unless it was a gift.

Their relationships seemed always to contain this evasion. My father and his father. My father and grandfather and grandmother. Grandmother and grandfather. By extension, myself and my grandparents. Money was a thing to be hidden, not spoken of above a whisper. In their world, if you showed you had money, people would give you less. If you admitted to having spent any, they would withhold their gifts. From grandfather to father and I was expected to take my part.

We continue driving south, passing the Palm Beach County line. West Palm Beach, Boynton Beach, and it's time to call my father and ask where to meet. Get off on Atlantic, left, Military trail, left. Look for the post office, left. Into High Point. Second stop sign, left, right. I call my daughter as she asked. She wants to go, for her grandfather. For her grandmother and for me but not for anyone

Funeral, Expurgated

else. She will not go until she knows I am there. I call her and she drives over from not far away. Boca Raton to Delray. From the mouth of the rat to the place of the kings. What does not sound better in Spanish?

I have parked but I do not know which condo it is. There are eight. Four in one section and four in another at right angles. All identical at this reasonable distance. I call my father to have him come out. I see him emerge from a corner unit and immediately begin to mouth words I cannot see.

He seems OK. I hug him and we enter the condo.

Once in I start to say hello. So does Alek. One by one. There is my uncle and his wife, Miral, a woman I have always liked. There is my aunt, Suki. There are some people I do not know. There is my mother. There is Erika, the caretaker, asking people if they want coffee, looking more after my mother than seems anyone else; Erika is the most animated person in the room and, other than my mother and myself, her French accent is the only speech that does not sound like New York.

There is my grandfather in the corner. My father is in the hallway mouthing words. I think he is telling me to say hello to everyone. Who can tell?

There is talk of the rabbi. Talk of the cantor. Who will do the service? My uncle is in from New Jersey. My aunt from Israel. My parents from down the road. Arrangements? No, it seems little has been done. A cantor has been called. Or a rabbi. I hear both terms over and over and she is due to arrive soon, was met with last night and is coming to help make arrangements.

They should be simple. A Jewish body is watched until it is in the ground. Prayers are said over it. My aunt and uncle are discussing the rules and traditions. I know as much about these as my uncle, and more than my aunt who claims to know all and makes up what she does not, usually with a fanciful mixture of myth and absurdity.

Some rabbis will not do the service because the body is not being buried in a completely Jewish cemetery. Problems, problems. I hear there is no casket available. I ask about this, knowing better. No casket is needed. The

Funeral, Expurgated

body is washed and watched by the *shomer*. It may be watched by family as well. Within twenty-four hours it is in the ground unless that places it on the Sabbath. Then two days. A burial shroud is used or a plain box with holes in the bottom so the body can touch the Earth.

One of the people I do not know states how disgusting that is. "But worms will touch the body!" Exactly. Don't hold on. Back to the Earth, back to dust.

My aunt talks about not holding on to the body, saying again and again, dust to dust, dust to dust.

So what is the problem with the casket? None needed. A plain one at best. We can build one from wood at a local lumber store. No nails may be used as it all has to disintegrate and decompose. Joints and glue. The casket was ordered? It is gold-colored, says my grandfather. It has to have a crown.

I am confused at the mix of steadfast faux tradition and disregard of the same. The discussion continues.

It won't touch the ground anyway, says my aunt. The casket will be in concrete, sealed.

My father says it is watertight. An non-embalmed body in a fancy wooden box in a sealed, water-tight concrete underground vault.

Why underground then, I ask.

"A Jew has to be buried underground." This I know.

My aunt continues to tell me, over and over, dust to dust, dust to dust. She'll have trouble getting there in an underground set of Chinese boxes.

Why are they having trouble finding a rabbi?

My daughter arrives. She says her hellos. People ask me if this is my wife.

She whispers to me asking where the body is. Is it in the bedroom? No. But who is watching it? Strangers, I say. People paid to watch.

My aunt and uncle talk in Hebrew. No one understands them. The make their purpose obvious: they talk in Hebrew, these two native citizens of the United States, so no one will understand them. They talk and point.

My uncle says he needs to cover the mirrors. Shiva lasts seven days and during this time the relations closest to the deceased do

Funeral, Expurgated

not shave, shower, groom or care for themselves. Food is brought in for them, cooked for them. All their time, for seven days, is spent thinking of themselves and their relation to the deceased. This is a breather. Time off from the cares of the world for the sons and daughters, the siblings, the spouse, the parents of the deceased. They sit on stools, tell stories, sleep, think.

Mirrors are covered so they may not be vain, seeing themselves unkempt, uncombed, unshaven.

My aunt immediately looks at my daughter, thinking she knows little and tells her the mirrors must be covered because the soul will wander the house and get confused. She has melded Hebrew burial traditions with feng shui, and my daughter tells her she is pretty sure it has to do with vanity and grieving.

The walls are mirrored.

We are waiting for the rabbi to arrive. Or the cantor. I hear both words mentioned again and again and do not know which to expect. It doesn't matter as either can perform a funeral by Jewish and state laws. She arrives and is asked to take a seat.

She introduces herself and is referred to as rabbi. She is middle-aged, well-spoken, conservatively dressed, and states she is a cantor. This is perfect, I think. The prayers will be sung instead of read, as they should be, as they were meant to be. She begins to detail plans. She is interrupted, in Hebrew.

My aunt and uncle are speaking Hebrew to talk to each in purposeful exclusion. My daughter, next to me, has remarked on the rudeness of this. This time it was ineffective. The cantor joined into the conversation. She is answered in English and my daughter whispers to me again, noticing the proof that these jaunts into Hebrew are no lapses but purposeful asides in front of their guests. My son has moved to the corner of the room, watching, quiet.

They have a problem with her—she is not a rabbi, but the cantor explains she can do a service as well by tradition and law. Not in an Orthodox service, is the quick retort by my aunt. The cantor mentions their service is not Orthodox. It is not in a Jewish cemetery, the body is in a fancy casket, it is in a vault. The conversation is fully, only, between

Funeral, Expurgated

my aunt and the cantor. Next to me, to my right, is my father. My uncle is across the small room next to my aunt. Next to my aunt, facing her, is the cantor. She is saying this:

"There are rules and then there are ways around the rules if you don't like them. In my tradition we do not pretend to follow the rule and then find a way around it. We follow it or we don't. This is not an Orthodox funeral. I am qualified. I have already done four this week so if you don't want me to do this that is fine. You simply have to tell me. Now, if there is another reason you are not comfortable using me, please tell me now."

"You are a woman."

"What does that have to do with it?" is what the cantor asks. No matter. She stands and thanks them. She is upset. They knew she was a woman. They spoke with her on the phone. They knew she was a cantor or thought she was. At any point they could have called and confirmed her position in the religious community.

"I can give you the names of some other people you might be interested in asking but I would not wait."

"Where are you going?" My aunt motions her to a seat again. "We don't charge for seats."

"You have made it clear you do not want me to perform this so there is no reason for me to be here."

"Please, have a seat," answers my aunt, slowly. "Let us figure this out."

She sits again. They talk a while longer. It becomes clear the funeral will not be tomorrow. It will be the day after. Friday morning at eleven. I excuse myself, stating I need to get something from my truck, and I walk out the door, into the parking lot.

Soon I am followed by my daughter. She asks me if I really needed something from my truck. She knows the answer. I walk over to my truck box, open it, pull out a box of my business cards and remove a quarter inch, ten or fifteen cards.

"See? I needed these," I say, holding them up and smiling at her. My daughter is shrewd and there is nothing she does not see through.

My son comes walking out. He says they are nuts. He has never seen anyone treated so rudely. This is a bad example for him.

Funeral, Expurgated

I want to apologize to her, for this treatment. I am used to it. She may not be. We wait.

Soon, we walk back to the condo and the open door.

I hear, as I approach, my aunt. "When do we need to let you know by if we decide to use you?"

"By the time I leave here. I'm not a yo-yo." The cantor gets up and walks toward the door.

"No, no. Have a seat. We want to know what to expect when we find a rabbi."

"You'll have to ask them," she says and does not stop, walks by us as she exits, heads into the parking lot to find her car.

"I'm sorry," I say to her back as she passes.

She keeps walking. "They're nuts," she responds, continuing on. Obviously she is not used to being treated this way and she has lost some of the composure she came in with. She slows and turns. Looks at me.

"You can see why I don't visit often," I say.

She walks to her car a few feet away and gets in. "I can fully understand it," she says, and shuts the door. We turn toward the condo.

Inside they are complaining that she misrepresented herself as a rabbi, that a cantor would not do. I take my seat as before, so does Sef. Alek takes a seat as well. I listen.

Over to my father, to my right, I lean. I whisper that no one has taken into account what my grandmother would have wanted. They argue, but not one person asks this question. He agrees this is a good point and asks me to say something. I tell him I'd rather not. I'd rather he say it. If I say it, there will be yelling.

"What?" asks my aunt. She has been prattling on in Hebrew but can't abide being left out of a conversation. My father tells her, tells everyone I have made a good point. That we should listen. I state, aloud, I'd rather not.

"Speak," she says. "We want to listen." I am prodded and finally do.

"I do not hear anyone asking or talking about what grandma would have wanted. You are arguing over a rabbi while letting other traditions go. As you argue, the time to burial gets longer and longer. What did she want? What does grandpa want?

Funeral, Expurgated

My aunt responds, loudly. She talks about how things are in Israel and still this has no bearing, seems to prove my point. No casket, she says. In twenty-four hours, she says. She says it is—and here she tosses in a Hebrew phrase—and then continues to talk in English but it makes no sense, disjointed as it is by a set of words I do not understand.

"Wait. I do not understand Hebrew. If you are going to talk to me it has to be in English."

"I am speaking English. I didn't speak in Hebrew." She is raising her voice steadily with each sentence.

"Excuse me, but one thing I do know is English and that was not English." Here I repeat the words in sounds as close as I can. My uncle says she did not notice she used it, used to it as she is.

"That's fine," I say. "That I understand, but please don't dismiss what I've said. Consider that if I said you did, I probably know English from Hebrew."

She continues to talk, loudly, about Hebrew. Sometimes in Hebrew. No one says anything. I look at my father and say, aloud, "This is why I didn't want to say anything." I get up. It is about four in the afternoon. I have had enough.

Outside, myself, my children, we talk about where to go for dinner. My father follows and plans are made for dinner. All I want is quiet and a salad. Really, just the quiet would do.

Lee calls. She has arranged to be here tomorrow and should arrive by eleven. My mother will need her. I know this. Will I? Doubtful. Doubtful.

The next morning I wake early from my daughter's couch, dress, walk. I eat breakfast, vegetable juice and herring I picked up the night before. Alek has eggs. My daughter has taken the day off. I call my father to find what time I should head up to Delray.

He'll call me back soon. In a half hour. He is closing on a house, finalizing a contract. I'm not sure. I am supposed to wait.

We do. An hour. Two hours. It is nearing noon. We get ourselves ready to go. Repeated phone calls are not answered and we leave.

A half hour later, nearing my grandfather's condo, my phone rings. I am turning into the complex. You are leaving there? I'm just arriv-

Funeral, Expurgated

ing? Why didn't you call and tell me? No, I'm not going to turn around and meet you at your house. That's an hour the other way now. I hate driving here.

I pull in and we walk up to the condo. My father is outside. He is mouthing something. I think it has to do with going out for dinner but not telling anyone. Why? We don't need to eat? Oh, with my brother and Amy. Why the secrecy?

Inside the house has been wrapped like a large roast from a butcher shop. It is all white paper on every mirrored surface. White butcher paper to the left and right. White butcher paper behind me. Directly in front of me, the glass cupboard reflects the entire room and I see myself, my children.

I say hello to everyone, hug my mother, my grandfather. There are people here I did not meet yesterday. People my age, younger. My cousins Duvid and Rom. Duvid comes over to say hello and introduces me to his wife, Arial, a gloriously charming and delightful woman. She is an acupuncturist in Hoboken and I know Lee will wish to meet her. Duvid is introduced to Sef and Alek. Erika asks if we want anything. Yesterday the coffee had no caffeine. Today, she whispers, she made caffeinated. Indeed, yes, please.

Sef, Alek, Duvid, and I talk about music. Duvid is a guitarist and has an artist's soul. We discuss playing alone versus playing with and how sharing musical space is so hard for some who emphasizes personal ability over art. He and Alek discuss rock and Arial and I gab about New York, medicine, organic foods, health. She is a pleasure to talk with. They both are. I haven't seen Duvid in nearly a decade. Before that, once. It was an afternoon when I diligently worked at convincing him he did not need his pacifier.

Duvid and Rom are not the cousins I hear of all the time. They are not the ones I was regaled about, compared to, measured against. There is no resistance here. We trade emails, phone numbers. Look at the butcher shop walls.

"It looks like we could sell add space. Or we should all autograph it."

There is agreement. I pull out my pen and write, tiny, at the very top corner in a space of less than half an inch, "Adam was here."

Funeral, Expurgated

From a foot away, it is hard to see it as anything but a mark on the stark white. My uncle walks over, looks up and says, "Discreet." It is. My name. Unobtrusive. Hardly there. Apparently easy to forget.

The day wears on and groups have formed. The siblings are off in corners discussing wills and arrangements. It seems continuous but more so regarding the disbursal of money, the purchase of the building than the burial of the body. Through this I hear snippets but try to not listen. Each person having received forty-two thousand, grandkids getting this or that, grandpa's new Lexus immediately switched with one of the kids for his old one.

Through it all one person has not stayed long in any group. Everyone seems to know him but me and my kids. Irwin.

He appears to be in his seventies. Tall, broad, white-haired. He seems nice. He seems gentle. Who is he? I ask. Grandma's brother married a girl, she died. This was their son. Soon after, he married his sister-in-law and then, sometime later, the brother died. Does that make Irwin my cousin? I think so. He talks with my parents before coming over to me. We speak. He seems oblique in his questions though fully friendly and comforting in a way no one else has been. He alone either does not know there is nothing to comfort or he alone needs comforting and has generalized that to me. To all.

The day moves on and we cousins talk more. No other cousins will be coming in. I shall not meet any of those I am held in comparison to. They will not come.

The funeral is at eleven tomorrow. We are asked to meet here at nine as that is when the limo arriving. I am not the only one asking why we're all meeting here if the limo will only hold the siblings and husband. Most of us state we'll be at the cemetery by eleven.

Evening is coming. It is nearly five and my daughter is hungry. My son is hungry. I probably am as well. My father mouths something and I tell him he'll have to break tradition and at least whisper instead. He tells me they will leave first and then we can leave but don't make it look suspicious. That we'll have dinner with "your brother" and Amy. They leave.

What is long enough to not look suspicious? What else am I supposed to do, and what is

Funeral, Expurgated

wrong with going out to eat with my brother? There is no food in the house so everyone here is going out, as far as I can see. Frankly, no one seems to care.

A few minutes later my cell phone rings. It is my father giving me instructions. I ask, "Which way do I drive?" and immediately he tells me, "Don't use the word 'drive.'"

I have walked toward the front window. Out of earshot? Probably not.

He tells me, "If you use the word 'drive,' they'll know you're going somewhere. Walk over to the window."

"How did I get here? Of course I'm driving. Do you think someone will decipher a diabolical dinner plan from me asking what direction to drive, considering I don't live here and drove two hours from Palm Bay?"

"I'm going to call Dana and find out where they want to go. I'll call you back. Stay put till then."

We say our goodbyes and leave. In the car I call Dana. My father wants us to drive to his house and go from there because he wants to cruise around and look for a place we'd all like. That sounds like a warmed up version of Hell; Ft. Lauderdale traffic, back seat car sickness, and squabbling over what place is healthy and what place not. I suggest just picking a place and meeting. We agree this is a far better option and he suggests the Cheesecake Factory. Just tell me where it is. Where? That far? What time?

Sawgrass Mills: third largest mall in the US. From the air it is shaped like an alligator. From the inside it is shaped like a mall. We are a bit early. We find the Cheesecake Factory and I walk inside to use the restroom leaving Alek and Sef outside in the courtyard of the Oasis section next to the Blue Dolphin entrance or the Pink Flamingo lot or something like that. When I come out everyone is there, gabbing about who was there today. I ask, "So what was up with Duvid getting married and no one getting an invitation?" Several people gasp, "Oh Geez," and my brother says that's why he doesn't give them any more than a hello and a goodbye.

"We just finished talking about that," he says.

"I'm sorry. How the hell was I supposed to know? It was an innocent question. The way

Funeral, Expurgated

people run their lives in *that* family" (I am careful to say "that"), "I figured their wedding was the last thing under their control. I'm careful not to judge intent. I was just curious."

"Well, I don't want to talk about it" is his immediate reply.

Lee and I eloped. Actually, we reverse-eloped. My parents said they'd throw us a wedding if her parents weren't invited. Her parents said they'd throw a wedding if I wasn't invited. We waited for a weekend both sets were out of town and got married.

There wasn't even an announcement for my brothers. Not that I recall. I never thought about that. Not until now.

We hear our last name and file in.

It is eight-thirty in the morning. I am putting on the best I have and so is Alek. I had dress black pants, but Alek needed a pair for something and by the end of the evening he had ripped them beyond repair. Sef's best is much better. South Florida has far better thrift stores.

We are into her car, feeling late at ten o'clock. Driving up 95, we exit at Hypoluxo Road, go too far by three miles into Lantana, turn around, find the correct road and the cemetery with its length directly boarding the highway. It is ten-thirty. We have not eaten and drive a mile the opposite direction looking for something I want but should not have. A bagel.

We finally come across a Dunkin Donuts and, in a place you would think would be rife with delis, it is the best we have found. Inside. It is crowded to its seeming capacity on this Friday morning and we each get coffee. I get a bran muffin, not giving in to my wants, and each of the kids gets their bagel. Dana calls. How far away is it? What road is it on? Join us, I say. We are five minutes away but there seems to be too little time and we finish our breakfast and drive back to the cemetery.

Pulling in at ten till eleven I see no cars we recognize. I park by the tent, as directed. The first tent. There are three. When my father said, "We'll be at the tent," I knew that would

Funeral, Expurgated

be problematic. I asked which tent and he told me there would be only one. One? "Do they only bury one person a day?" I asked. This was a fair question, asked in an unfair way, I grant. But this was the man who once hit me for insisting he was wrong when I asked what flavor ice cream was with no flavoring added. "Vanilla," I was told. I said vanilla was a flavor. Wouldn't it taste just like milk? For some reason that deserved my being slapped. I learned to ask questions in unfair ways.

We walked and found workers, asked them where Tritt was and they pointed to the large building close to the wall that divided those who had already found death from the eight lanes of those speeding toward it.

We walked. We entered. Lee called. She had called several times that morning, while we were waking, showering, dressing, to tell us she would be late, each time keeping me on the phone as I tried to rise, shower, or dress, telling me in great detail why she would not be there on time. Finally, I said it was OK. She had no need to call to tell me she would be late as a device to take up time so she would be late. It was a trip, for her, of just over one-and-a-half hours.

So she called Sef. Sef was not as charitable and told her squarely if she got off the phone and stopped complaining about being late, she'd have been on her way. But what does she wear? It doesn't matter. Bring clothes for later, yes.

Now we are waiting at five minutes to eleven and Lee tells me where she is, that she may be late. I let her know she is fewer than five minutes away and I will wait for her. Two men in black suits tell me the "family" is in the office and will enter together. More people arrive. Lee arrives, hugs me, and walking the long hall between the twenty-foot walls of vaults, we go in.

In the front of the hall is an ornate, gold-toned casket. To the right of it, in the corner, is the lectern. There are seven rows of seats and ten seats to a row. The first row is empty, the second mostly full, the third, full from the far end halfway in. Behind, they are empty. In the last of the half-full row is my brother and we take our seats—I next to my brother

Funeral, Expurgated

and Lee next to me. Alek and Sef sit in front of us with their second cousins.

I look for my mother and do not see her. Then, I do, at the end of the second row, thin, in a cap, small and frail, she looks to be a little boy. Next to her is Erika.

There is talking, quiet laughter, joking. Is she missed? It is hard to say. Not by her grandchildren, it would seem. At least not by all. Not by her great-grandchildren.

The two men in the black suits enter and ask all to stand for the family. We do and they enter, single file, my grandfather at the lead, on a cane, then my aunt, my uncle, and my father, last. They sit. We sit. The rabbi enters.

He is dressed in black, black and black topped with a wide-brimmed black fedora. Behind the lectern he stands and starts by opening his mouth and pausing, says he did not know the deceased, pauses, looks at his notecard, and says, slowly, "Mrs. Tritts."

He is corrected by a voice from the assembled. "Tritt." But there are four Mrs. Tritts in the room: three living. One Mrs. Tritt not present. One Mrs. Tritt to be and one Miss Tritt. I look around and see I am not the only person to notice this. I look at Lee and, turning, find her eyes instantly.

He continues to call her Mrs. Tritt, eulogizing five women in one. He talks to us about her being a daughter of the Jews and his sister and, therefore, knows her just the same. His sister, Mrs. Tritt. He starts with the prayers.

He reads them in English quickly. So quickly I can barely follow. He then says them in Hebrew because, he tells us, the soul understands its native language best. He says them at a speed that is ferocious and fluid so there are no divisions between the words, no melody, no rhythm. These are prayers and he says them as though they are a pharmaceutical insert, skimming out loud in search of some hidden important information. They are songs that he reads like dosage instructions. He reads from the *Song of Songs* even faster as though there is a schedule to keep and melody would only serve to slow things down, beauty would only get in the way.

He calls up Irwin to give a eulogy. He has cards—prepared, he says, so he would not falter. He means it. He means everything he says and it is all beautiful. He doesn't look at the

Funeral, Expurgated

cards, cries, talks about that which is lost, how good and kind she was, his love for his aunt, the matriarch of the family, her strength, her support. He means every word and I hold tears but they are not for her. They are not for her.

I turn and Lee is looking at me. She quietly says she has no idea who he is talking about but it isn't the woman she knew. It isn't the woman I know either. Not at all. She holds my hand. Irwin steps from the lectern, shaking his head. "I just loved her, is all. I just loved her," as he moves to his seat. And the service ends.

The two men in black tell us it is time. We are to move to the graveside, at the tent. The family can take the limousine. The kids and I walk with Lee and Erika pushing my mother in turns. In two minutes we are at the grass and across a short field of six by twelve inch bronze plaques laid flat upon the ground, marking the heads of graves.

In the green field is a reflection of stark gray marble slabs longer each than a body, wider than a coffin, nine widths long and two across: an interruption of cloud in the grass. All but the last one, the side close to us. It is open and concrete. Next to it, the tent. About fifty feet further to the right a dull yellow backhoe. On the grass, attached to its shovel, by four taut chains, is a concrete slab and next to it, a marble one: another cloudy hole in the green earth. And all around, six by twelve bronze place-markers of people who were.

My mother stays at the roadside with Erika. We walk to the tent. There are folding chairs beneath it, three rows of six, and they sit on several pieces of plywood. Everyone sits. In the front row, my grandfather, my aunt, my uncle, and my father.

The casket arrives on a draped cart pushed by men in blue workshirts. The cart is positioned over the open bunker and the drapes hide the hole beneath. The rabbi starts rapidly again and a switch is moved on the cart. The coffin descends slowly to settle into the pit.

Sef has stayed with me the entire time. My son, no further than arm's reach. Lee at my side. My brother close. They all retreat. Lee tells me she is going to go stay by my mother,

Funeral, Expurgated

that she needs her and I have no doubt she is right.

I am by the grave, by myself except for the workers. Watching.

They move mechanisms at the wheels and the cart unlocks itself from the grave, is pulled away. The rabbi continues, holds a baggy of dirt from Israel so that the daughter of Zion can be buried in Jewish soil, in Florida, in this bunker, covered in marble. The workers leave.

The two men in black tell me I must move. Those seated under the tent, milling, pacing, they must move. The tent must move as well. The backhoe rumbling, suddenly, and the slab is leaving the ground, swinging from the bucket by its chains.

The tent is picked up and walked by its four corners, the chairs are taken away and I help fold them. The plywood is relocated from the graveside to in front of the backhoe tracks. More plywood, uncovered as the top sheets are removed, are relocated as well, making a narrow road for the tracks from where it sits to the vault.

I look into the hole. It is not right that she is not buried, that the full measure of soil there is only a baggy of Holy Land. There is no shovel. There is no pile of soil. I ask the rabbi, "Is it alright if I throw some dirt in? It doesn't feel right if I don't." His answer is, "Of course."

I crouch over the grave, look down, reach to my right and grab a handful of sandy soil, talk quietly, drop grit as I speak.

"I don't know why you never treated us the way you treated everyone else. Apparently you were very good to many people. I don't understand. But I thank you for what you did give me. You showed me how not to treat people. I know how to be good and kind because you showed me what it was like when someone isn't. How much it hurts. And thank you. If not for you, I wouldn't have Sef or Alek. Here. Here is the only dirt in your grave by a relative. Just me. Goodbye."

And with that, my handful rains down. I stand up, stand back as the men in the black suits ask me to watch out. Here comes the slab.

Funeral, Expurgated

As I back up, Irwin comes up to me. I think of his words. My eyes begin to tear. "Everyone will miss her," he says, and puts his hand on my shoulder.

I am surprised to be talking to him. I am surprised to be crying.

"That's not why I'm crying." I say this and am shocked I have spoken but more so over what words have come out, that I am being honest. I continue as he looks at me. "I hear how good she was to everyone and how wonderful and I want to know how come I was cheated out of that. Why did she treat us so badly? Why did everyone get this loving grandmother and we got nothing. I'm crying for me. Not her."

He apologizes to me. He means it. Not for how I feel, but for his lack of understanding, for her. He continues. "I don't know why she treated you the way she did. She wasn't like that with anyone else but you and your brother and your mother. Your mother is a wonderful person. I know her and Franky a long time and I never understood it." This he says shaking his head. "It was unfair and I never understood it."

I appreciate this and he leaves me with a hug. My tears become sparse as my brother approaches to me. Irwin spoke with him as well and the conversation, while ending the same way, started quite differently. He had no idea who we were. We were never mentioned. Not by the grandparents. Not by my parents. Not in his memory.

He was amazed to see not because he was surprised at our presence but at our existence. After stepping on that with my brother, he was kind enough not to repeat it to me. That I found out later is of no consequence to his kindness and I will always appreciate his candor and restraint in a time of such difficulty for him.

I am shocked. How does a parent not mention their children? In forty-two years? My tears dry. They are used up. I am empty and, suddenly, much more alone.

The backhoe is over the grave, the lid, swinging, guided by workers, descends and my father talks to the men in the black suits about the guarantee of watertightness of the vault. They explain there is no such guarantee. There never was one and especially not

Funeral, Expurgated

in Florida. Gaskets? No. Seal? No. His face drops. He wants her sealed and safe. Permanent.

I think fallout shelter. I think Ziplock. Tupperware.

One blue work shirt leans over to adjust the top so it lowers just right. He jumps into the vault to undo the chains and the backhoe retreats, beeping.

As it does, the driver misses the plywood and runs over plaque after plaque, hitting the corners, pressing them into the ground as they pop catercornered into the air one after another until the row becomes a line of bronze diagonals. I had been doing my best not to step on the head-plaques.

Now comes the marble cover. It too is brought over at the expense of plaques and noise and I watch it put into place, positioned perfectly before I walk away. All is done.

Erika will drive the van back. My mother will ride with Lee. I have the kids. All back to my grandfather's house. Twelve-thirty.

Once back, Erika is busy putting the food out, all cakes and sweets. I was told I need not bring anything. Nothing was needed or wanted. Food is supposed to be supplied for the people sitting shiva. I should have brought food anyway.

Here are cakes. Cookies. Breads and crackers. No food to sustain. Here are also cardboard boxes printed to look like wooden benches for the family to sit on. Within the hour my father has crushed one under him. Cakes, cookies, and breads.

My brother walks by me, asks quickly, quietly for whom the funeral we attended was for. He did not know that woman either. He walks on.

We talk. I introduce my wife to Arial and they talk shop at the table about their practices, laws, medicine, and get along well. There is wine and my aunt drinks one, two three cups nearly immediately. I know this because she counted them out loud and had five within the next two hours. It showed.

Erika is busy, stays busy, out of the way. The siblings have moved to the far, deep corner of the kitchen and are discussing in hushes. We talk with the cousins. There are others.

Soon, my aunt is drunk, the conversation is loud, my wife and children are hungry. It

Funeral, Expurgated

is nearly five in the afternoon. I say my goodbyes. Hug my mother, my father. Take my cousin's email addresses and phone numbers, thank Irwin, and say goodbye to Erika. We head to Lee's sisters where we will spend the night.

We change. Where to go for dinner? The Whale's Rib in Lighthouse Point, but five minutes away from the house. It is crowded, inexpensive, comfortable and, I think, what we need this evening. We sit, wait for our table and talk.

I ask Lee questions. I ask how parents neglect to ever tell relatives about their children, how a grandparent treats some grandchildren well and leaves others ignored.

I tell her, today, I feel cut loose. Today, I have less of a family behind me. Today, less of a family in my past, that fewer people care. I feel I was deluded. I feel the family I have chosen, a blessing, and those I was born with . . . I do not finish. I do not know how I feel. Maybe I do and don't want to say.

I know my father as weak. Did he ever talk about the lack of parity? He seemed, always, to simply accept all as it was, to question nothing his family did. Perhaps this is unfair. I don't know. I have been undefended, unmentioned, unknown. As though I was not there.

We sit. Lee talks to me and I am glad of it. I listen closely and ask her to write down what she has told me. I want to see it, to read it, again and again. To know it was not just me. She did and I include it here. It is a bit more than I had anticipated. It is unedited.

> I felt I needed to add my two cents to your essay. I was a participant also.
>
> How sad for her. How much hate can cheat you out of life. This poor, ignorant woman who was afraid her daughter-in-law was after her money cheated herself out of life's joys and died bitter and hating. Although she lived to a very ripe old age of 94, she cheated herself from knowing and loving not only her grandchildren, but her great-grandchildren. How horribly sad for her. In her worry about being robbed, she not only

Funeral, Expurgated

cheated herself, but three generations behind her. She cheated my husband and his brother from having a grandmother who loved them. They also cheated themselves out of knowing their children, grandchildren and great-grandchildren. How sad is that?

My children, her great-grandchildren, who are lucky enough to know their great-grandparents, do not like them. They are duly compensated, however, in having the loving grandparents that my husband and his brother do not.

So who did she hurt with her hate? Let's see... her son, his wife, and their two sons. But the list does not end here. It also includes others in the family who are baffled by this hatred. The non-understanding that was prevalent at her funeral. Questions unanswered as to why this had occurred.

Uneasiness all around by the few other friends and family members who showed up.

I think there were six of them.

Erika was not in the kitchen the entire time. Part of the time she spent with Lee. Upset, she needed someone to talk with, to vent to. She knows Lee. Lee is not part of the family. Not by blood. Erika knows how she feels and Lee is safe.

Erika is angry. She ranted on and on about how the brother and sister treat my father like a dog. Dog is the word she used. Over and over. As we wait near the bar, Lee goes on, more and more. She needs this off her, out of her.

Erika was there when grandmother died. She was there for her last words.

Grandpa came near. To him she says, "I always knew you'd steal my money."

And then, "Get away from me, you bastard."

And she died.

There is a break at the bar. They have Guinness on tap. It is four dollars and a quarter a

Funeral, Expurgated

pint. Four and a quarter and far too many calories. I don't actually need this. I order one.
   The cliff is always closer than it appears.

Passover and the Industrial Revolution

Every Passover I bake matzah.
I wait until there is
Nothing left to do,
I wait for the lull
In the torrent of business and busyness
And preparation for the unexpected
  guest,
The soup is bubbling slowly
Covered, tzimmes done,
Choroseth setting
And Passover plate
Covered, in the fridge
Next to the gefilte fish.

When there is nothing left to do
And everything is finished

I bake
I work as quickly as I can
Rushing, like of old
When there was everything to do
And nothing to be done but hurry.

I work to make bread
Matzah shemurah,
"Watched matzah"
As of old,
Before the machines were invented,
Before 1857 and the mixers and
   kneaders,
Rollers and perforators of the
Industrial Revolution.
In fewer than eighteen minutes
From flour to done,
Nothing can rise
But the realization of the mitzvah,
Purpose for preparation,
Intention
And prayers.

At a temperature I can comfortably
   reach my hand into
They bake.
Quickly

Passover and the Industrial Revolution

Like bare feet on desert sand.

When they are done
They have opened in the
Center, crisp and brown,
Heavy and thick,
Empty. Receptive . . .

This is not like the matzah
From a box.
My matzah is not a gigantic saltine
Stacked like x-ray plates
Or cards
Or slates.
Although . . .

When I was seven
I went on a field trip
Through the Jersey countryside
To the clogged vessels of
Dense New York streets,
Sitting in the Yeshiva bus,
Staring down
At the faces in the unmoving cars
We slid, heated, halting,
Metal to metal cells, fuming forward.
Finally, stilled, we gratefully

Disembarked, stood and walked along

Delancey Street
The lower east side
Of Manhattan,
With my school class,
We visited a temple during minyan
Sat separated
Girls from boys
On an austere balcony of
Dark woods and dark ages
Staring above the vaulted steps
At the dais of black-coated men
Listening to the song to their beloved
Carried with the audible overtone of
　the holy
And an undertone of confidence
The song was surely heard.

We were there for days or minutes
And fidgeted, fussed, squirmed
In the presence of the Universal King.
After, released of our confinement
Reconfined to sturdy lines to walk
On to the great mystery of the
Matzah factory.

Passover and the Industrial Revolution

Past the pickle barrels
On the sidewalks
Where for ten cents
We all got to dip our hands
And pull a half-sour
From the briny cask,
Close by,
And brick-built
Red and high-windowed
Was the matzah factory.

We entered though the loading dock
And never wondered if there was
A door, an office, a warehouse but
There were ovens
Vast and hot.

We stood on a balcony
Over the open factory floor,
Vats and vaults
Mixers and all over the smell of flour.
Rolling from the vat,
Poured onto a sheet, rolled into the ovens
Pressed by combs
For perforation
For ease of use

For profit
For Horowitz-Margareten,
Streits, Manischewitz
The Matzah Monopoly
For tables during Passover
For people to gingerly, slowly shop for
In Pathmark, Shop-Rite, Foodtown
Kids in cart, mamma picking her box
Of matzah, plums, salami
And, if she was in a hurry
It had nothing to do with
Evacuation, or the Pharaoh
Or Moses except that
We'd read it in the Haggadah
And break the matzah,
Ask the questions, dip the
Parsley, spread the horseradish
And bite.

The factory was hot with baking
And we left, sweating, drenched
Flour-powdered without and
Within, samples of matzah,
In a single-file exodus from the ovens.
Which, every Passover
I recreate in my kitchen.

Passover and the Industrial Revolution

The bread of affliction
Is my joy, my revolt,
My exodus and cry unto the
　wilderness
To my own kind—
"Let my people go."

The Harmony of Broken Glass

A million years ago, I used to own a bookstore. The community had asked for it and even put up much of the money. In return, they'd receive a return on their investments when the store turned a profit and would have a local store that carried the things they wanted. All Lee and I did was to quit our jobs, invest our time and money, and pour our hearts and souls into it. They gave us a list of the sorts of things they wanted, we stocked them, and they pointed their browsers at Amazon to buy the books and drove to Wal-Mart to buy the candles and soon we were out of business and they could not quite figure out why.

We were in Gainesville, Florida, at the end of Sixth Street, where it met 441 at an acute angle just past the north side of town. Our building was an old gas station built in 1906. It had the original brick foundation holding up the original cedar beams holding up the original pine tongue and groove floors holding up the original pine tongue and groove walls in which were held the original windows. Nearly one hundred years old the entire building was, and it creaked and groaned and loved every step made inside.

The building had two main rooms. The front, the salesroom, was twenty by twenty and windows all around except for the front door on the south wall perpendicular to the street, and the door leading to the second room, right in the middle of the west wall with a large pane of glass, door to wall, on either side. The second room, twenty by forty, was solid wall on the north and east. Separated by glass from the front room and, on the south side, made of century old wood, plaster and glass. Mostly glass.

The windows were high and wide with broad sills. In the second room, three of them stretched from the front to the back. As one looked to the lower edges of any of the windows, as one looked to the grass below through the bottom of the pane, the world stretched, became bulbous, swirly. If you put your hand on the glass, you could feel it thicken as one got closer to the sill. Thin at top and thick at the bottom. Old poured glass windows—a super-viscous liquid that slowly, over nearly one hundred years, poured towards its own bottom. Kids would love to sit there and stare though the bottom and watch the world wiggle, fatten, and wave. So did I.

This was the room we used for classes and workshops. Around its perimeter, it held rugs and t-shirts, dresses and scarves as well as other textiles, folded on tables, hung from frames, and tacked to the walls. So large, it was, we never had to move anything much for a workshop or fair.

We had bands too, and we'd serve coffee. We'd be open until eleven and many of the coffee drinkers would not purchase anything, so we figured the coffee would pay for the electric that evening, at the least. The coffee was in the small kitchen area off the large room and it was self-serve, as we were neither set up nor licensed for food service.

At first it was by donation. When we found the donation can with little money but filling fast with empty sugar packets and gum wrappers, we decided the honor system wasn't working and charged a dollar for the cup. Not the coffee. Just the cup. All our mugs went behind the front counter. Folks could ask for one, pay their buck, and drink all night if they wanted. On an average night we should have made thirty to fifty bucks from the folks who otherwise would not have spent a cent. Folks who came in and bought books and such, we'd happily hand a cup to. Everyone gets to do their share.

It wasn't long before I started seeing people walking around with coffee in vessels I had never seen before. Little ones. Big ones, Even stainless steel thermoses and double-size travel cups. I'd ask for the buck for the night's coffee and they'd show me their one quart mason jar, telling me they had brought it from home so no need to hand any cash over to me. I suggested, along with the cup, next time they should bring their own coffee, too. Late nights at the bookstore ended soon after that.

But the workshops continued. Authors, therapists, artists. Book talks, dances, songfests. I taught a few myself, on occasion.

I had, over the few years prior, been doing a workshop on chants from the Kabbalah. I had been doing them at the local Unitarian Universalist Fellowship, at churches as far away as Greensboro, North Carolina, in the forests of Ohio, and even in a hot tub. So why not do one at my own store?

The night was set and we had a very nice turnout of over thirty people. Someone volunteered to watch the register and I set to work. Three rules only. These rules, along with the chants themselves, were taught to me by Rabbi Shelly Isenberg, who was the Chair of the University of Florida Department of Religion. They seemed to work for him, and they work for me.

Three rules:

- ✦ Everyone stands who is able to stand. "I'm tired" is not a reason for not standing. We always lose a few at this one. People walk out in a huff because they aren't going to be able to sit and chant.

No full breaths from a full body while sitting curled in a chair.

- ✦ Everyone singing. No gawkers. We always lose a few more at that. When I tell them we'll be chanting for an hour or so, still more leave. I tell them it won't feel like an hour. That they will wonder where the time went but people want fast, instant results and they want them easy. They want to slouch in a chair and attain enlightenment from watching other people sing for five minutes. Good luck.

- ✦ The last rule is everyone comes to the center. I set up four chairs in the middle of what will be our circle and, at some point, each person comes to the center to sit and have the rest of us sing around them, letting them feel the sound, the vibration, the harmony. I often have a person help me make sure everyone gets their chance. I joke that I call her my shill. I tell them, at some point, I'll be going to the center as well and, please, please, they should not stop chanting just because I have. Always people laugh at this. The twenty or so people who remained did exactly that—laughed. The group had been culled and we were ready to start.

The chants are short and simple. We learned the first one by listening to me say it once, then the group repeating after me. Then saying it with me. Then I sing it on my own and we sing it once together. That's it. No lengthy process. Nothing written on paper until the end of the workshop. The first time I taught this I passed out the chants, with their translations, on paper before we started. Then, with the chants written down, people read them over and over instead of singing, looking at the paper the entire time.

People worried about losing the words. They always do. Don't worry, I tell them. There is power in the tune itself. Hum, tone, sing *dai de dai* like we have all heard rabbis do. The tunes have lasted a thousand years. Two thousand years. There is power in the sound. Never worry about the words.

We sang our first chant, all in our circle, four times. It was practice, it was invocation, it was lovely.

> Hineyni
> Osah (oseh) et atzmi
> Merkavah l'Sh'kinah
> Merkavah l'Sh'kinah

Hineyni is "here I am." *Oseh* (*Osah* for the guys in the group) *et atzmi* is "I make myself become." *Merkavah* is a chariot. *Sh'kinah* is, literally, the Presence, but a distinctly feminine manifestation of the divine presence, so "Goddess" is a good translation. But not a particular Goddess, however, and definitely not the word for small-g goddesses. That's what Craig R. Smith told me, at least. And I believe him.

Here's how Shelly translated it:

> Here I am!
> I make myself
> A chariot for the Goddess.

I like that. That's how I translated it then. That's how I translate it now.

We learned the next chant.

> Ana
> El na'
> R'fa na lah

That simple. I sing it once through before telling them what it means:

> Please
> Strong One, oh please
> Heal the world (all)(nature) please.

Here is what Craig says about it:

> *Ana* and *na'* both mean "please," loosely. It's somewhere between begging and pleading and a demand, so it's closer to "oh please, NOW!" *El*, one of the words translated "God," means "strong one." It's the same root as other strong words. For example, the word *ayil* is a ram (strong one of the flock), *ayal* is a stag (strong one of the forest) and *eyal* is strength. *R'fa* means "to heal." Tradition teaches that prayer need not be lengthy or elaborate. This is the earliest known

> Jewish prayer for healing, uttered by Moses as a petition on behalf of his sister, Miriam: "*El na, refa na lah*, God, please heal her, please." *Lah* is "her," and the Kabbalists say this is to be expanded to all of nature.

The chant is done four times, steady, rising, steady, falling, then starts over again, again, again, again, again. Ten minutes, twenty minutes. An hour. Voices rise and fall. Voices high and low. Melding, separating, harmonizing, combining into overtones that no single voice creates. A circle of sound as, one by one, two by two, people come to the center, sit, vibrate throughout, breathe, heal. And all the while, a sound around it all, a tone at once over the overtone and under the lowest voice. It permeates and surrounds and whence it comes we've no idea.

An hour. An hour and a quarter. An hour and a half and the chant slows, quiets, takes longer breaths, then ends all at once as if by a cue, unheard and unseen. Silence.

What did you experience? I saw the color blue everywhere. I could not stop singing. It

The Harmony of Broken Glass

was not my voice. I felt waves. I was connected. My body sang as I stood. I felt calm. Calm. No time passed.

Water passes around. Some sit, some pace. Some wonder what the sound was, that sound over the sound, that sound under the sound.

I walk to the far window, the window toward the back, for some space. To look out, to look down and see the grass wave through the thick glass and notice something new. Powder. Flakes. Chips on the wood sill. The caulking around the window is loose. The window, vibrating in the frame, has loosed the old glazing. The window, vibrating in the frame, sang.

We gather again to say goodbye. A short chant only, easy to learn and in English. We make two lines facing each other, close to each other, holding hands with the person to my right, holding hands with the person to my left, close enough to hug the person I am facing, each line joining hands at each end. We are a circle pressed to a double line. We look into each other's eyes and chant, then move to the right, look into another set of eyes, sing, move to the right.

> Come let us light up our hearts.
> Come let us light up our homes
> Breathe in,
> And breath out
> Making circles of love.
> Oh, come, let us light up the world.

Move to the right, look into those eyes, sing, move, look, sing. Her eyes, his eyes, my eyes.

Full circle. No one ends. We go round again. All is quiet. All is done.

The next day we came to the store a little before nine in the morning to discover the phone wasn't working. In the very back of the building was a large room, concrete floored, with a separate entrance. It appeared to be a machine shop from the old gas station days and one could not get to it from the inside. I walked there now, through the front room, through the large workshop area, past the small office in the back we rented to a fledgling acupuncturist, out the back door and around to the right. I knocked on the door. This was the landlord's office.

Michael Rose owned the building and the house next door. Actually, it was one property with two buildings. He also owned a New Age store not far from us. On top of these ventures, he was the US importer for Blue Pearl Incense. When he was in town he was a good landlord and a more than decent person. Usually, however, he was out of town. Often at an ashram in Sarasota or India or who knows. Today was unusual and he was in his office. But his phone was not working either. Together we walked around the building to look at the lines.

It was a calm summer. There was no storm the night before. And so we were quite surprised to see, before we ever got to the phone lines, a thick black wire hanging from the tall utility pole a few feet from our building lying slack from the roof.

The wires were intact leading to the house on the property, parallel to our store, so Michael knocked on the door to use their phone. The line from their roof was still attached to the pole. It was not long before a gentleman from the phone company arrived.

It didn't take him long to fix it though he had to run a new, longer line. That seemed a bit strange. Why not just attach the old one? Would making it longer keep it from breaking?

When I asked, with Michael looking up at the new line, the repairman just shook his head. He said the building had shifted nearly two inches and that had put enough strain on the line to pull it off. How it shifted, he'd no idea. He'd seen this after floods or, more rarely, large storms. Our area is not known for tremors and, if there had been one, certainly there'd been more lines pulled off than just ours.

He left. Michael shook his head. Tall, heavyset, usually smiling, he stared concerned up at the roof. I told him I thought I might know what happened and asked if he would come inside and look at a window.

I lead him to it and he immediately saw the flaked glazing and the powder on the sill.

"We had a chant workshop last night. We wondered what the buzzing was."

He breathed in heavily and out again, aiming at the window sill and blowing the powder into the air. He was more than familiar with chanting, with sound and with vibration. He also had been invited to participate. But, still I had not expected him to actually be happy.

But happy he was. His eyes squinted and his smile grew wide and he laughed.

"Fantastic. I wonder what other damage you guys did. Other than moving the building. Can you break it? Can you break the window?"

"I have no idea. Why would I?"

"Do it. Break the window next time. I'll replace it. It'll be worth it if you can do it. I want to see."

And so the next workshop was set but this time we called everyone we knew who would be the slightest bit interested. When they hesitated, I'd tell them the goal.

No, no charge. Just show up. Show up and sing.

Never underestimate the power of promised destruction. People came just for the opportunity to sing a window broken. People brought people. Small folk and thin folk with voices high and piercing. Big folk and squat folk with voices booming and deep.

More than forty people were there, in that room. We were not crowded and had space between us as we stood in one large oval. Four chairs were set in the middle. We were going to do this right.

Dusk came. Held in the air, a red thread could not be told from a blue one and so it was deemed night and we sang our invocation. It was livelier than usual but the invocation quieted the spirits and settled the energy.

Then, on to the chant. Many had been to the last workshop and knew the chant but we taught it from scratch. Why not? It doesn't take long and I wanted everyone to get as much out of this workshop as possible. If we didn't break a window, we should still all leave with something we learned and a story to tell.

> Ana
> El na'
> R'fa na lah.
> Ana

El na'
R'fa na lah.
Ana
El na'
R'fa na lah.
Ana
El na'
R'fa na lah.

Down low. Ascending. Up high. Descending. Down low. Ascending. Up high. Descending. Voices mixed, changed, created other voices. Forty felt like fifty, like eighty, sounded like a hundred. The space felt vast, the room felt small, people walked to the center, vibrated visibly, found harmonies. The pictures on the walls clattered. The hum was evident. Obvious. It was loud and came in waves, different this time. Higher, oscillating, changing. Was it one of the windows? Was it one of the two large panes of glass separating the rooms? Was it something else? No matter, we continued and continued and the sound gloried in its being sung.

Time past unnoticed, the ineffable cue was felt and we slowed, quieted, stopped. We sang our last chant, each looking into the eyes of the person across in a double serpentine bent at the walls. Again, it was quiet.

So quiet. We just stood there. No one wanting to talk. I asked no one to tell what they saw, felt, heard. I asked no one to share their experience. The silence told the story.

No one rushed to the windows.

But after a while I walked to the front window to look out and see the moon rising. I looked up to see it over the trees, bright and beautiful. I stood, staring through the window.

And what was this? In the high left corner, small small, a crack. Visible if one looked but nothing terribly noticeable. Still, a crack. We had done it. We broke the window. Not shattered, not busted, but broken nonetheless. In the end, I'm glad it was small. The perfect result in all ways. We did what we set out to do but the window could stay, as it had, for nearly a century. We could still see the grass wave, convoluted, from the thickened bottom. The glass, as originally placed, would continue on. Of that, too, I was glad.

The Harmony of Broken Glass

Because, if you get very close, if you listen very carefully and very near, on a quiet, quiet day, you can hear the recorded hundred years—the rumbling cars and trucks, shoes on raised wood floors, thunder and pelting rain, laughter, the harmony in the broken glass.

Fifty Years

Had I been born fifty years earlier
I would sit in a café in Paris,
Trade wit, find work writing copy
And critique, adventure in the arts
   and love,
Drink dark coffee and absinthe.

I would meet people in occluded
   rooms,
Crowded stations, and hush
Listen carefully, I will only say this once,
Pass small slips with single names,
Hide men in my attic,
Wonder about tomorrow.

Had I been born fifty years earlier
I would say the proper *brucha*
Each morning, listen to my papa,
Go to yeshiva, study Talmud,
Marry whom I was told.

I would look toward the steppes
And one day see the horses,
My small town in smoke,
My footprints and cart tracks behind
 me,
Hope for a ticket of passage,
Wonder about tomorrow.

Had I been born fifty years earlier
I would go to school
In the town with everyone else,
Shop in the markets,
Consider myself a citizen.

I would one day hear the crashing
 windows,
See the walls built, the paint flow,
The armbands and the army trucks,
Wonder what we had done,
Avoid the uniforms,
Wonder about tomorrow.

Yahrzeit

This, today, August 29th, 2010, is the one year anniversary of my mother's death. *Yahrzeit*.

I could not write this. But I could say this. I dictated it and a friend, a good friend, for who else would do such a thing, typed it while I talked. He also made what edits and proofs were needed. He did this to save me the pain of a careful reading. Thanks, Craig.

I read it anyway.

I do not say this is what happened. What is here is truth but may not be fact. It is what I remember from two days that are hard to remember. I have added things as I recall them. Still, maybe I got something wrong. Maybe I got something backward. Maybe I made a mistake. Maybe someone will be mad. Maybe they'll get over it. Maybe they won't.

It doesn't matter.

My brother called me that Thursday and told me my mother was in the hospital, or that she was going into the hospital, I actually don't quite remember which one. I said I would try to get down the next week or so, and he said he thought it was important I get down there in the next day and so. I left the next morning.

My mother had Parkinson's Disease, had it for about fifteen years. For the last two years she'd had trouble speaking, and she seemed more and more trapped. She had brain surgery, which really didn't work for much more than two or three weeks at a time. I think she hadn't walked in probably a good year.

So I called my daughter and asked Sef if I could stay with overnight at her place. She was living in Deerfield Beach and my mother was in the hospital in Coral Springs, about twenty minutes away. I also asked if she would meet me at the hospital. And she said of course she would. So I drive down and I got there around 11, and Sef met me outside

Yahrzeit

the hospital. And we walk in together. I think we met my brother on the way up to the room, or perhaps outside the room. Apparently my mother was not able to swallow anymore. I hadn't seen her in, I think, about two months. I had called from time to time, but because she was unable to speak, she would try to speak on the phone but end up crying, so I alternately thought I should just call and not have her talk, or I should not call so as to not make her cry. So I probably didn't call her as often as I might have. I certainly didn't call her as often as I wanted to, because the crying was hard for both of us. She was such a dynamic person, it was harder to hear her not be able to speak than it was to see her not able to move.

So we went in to see her. My father had called the night before my brother did, and he said she had not been eating, and I forget what else he said, but he was considering taking her to the hospital. I suggested he take her right away—from his description she needed to be there—but he was wondering, vacillating. I believe it was my brother who finally convinced him to get her to the hospital.

Went in. She really looked very "shell-ish," nearly unable to move, unable to eat because she couldn't swallow. I went in, gave her a hug, Sef gave her a hug, I did my best to not cry and I didn't. My father, of course, takes me outside immediately to talk to me "in secret"—he was always telling secrets, always took me aside to whisper things—"Your mother's not doing well, you're mother's not this or that," as if my father still thought she was 40 and playing croquet, as if it were to be a surprise to him that she's sick. When he'd call and say she's not getting better, I'd say, "What did you expect, this is what happens with Parkinson's." I think he was trying to hold on to her, but I found it frustrating. He would whisper it because he didn't want her to hear.

So I sat with her, held her hand, Sef was on the other side, held her hand, talked to her. She made a few sounds here and there, she could move her eyes a little bit. Apparently a Swallow Test had been ordered—I'm not sure what the logistics of a Swallow Test are, I really don't need to know—but they came and got her, wheeled her down, and before they wheeled her back up, I spoke with the

Yahrzeit

nurse and asked what the plan was, what the possibilities were. If the Swallow Test came out well, she would be able to eat. If the test did not come out well, she would be unable to eat, and the only way she would be able to receive nutrition would be through a tube going through her side and into her stomach. But the Parkinson's medications can only be administered orally. So it means the Parkinson's would get worse and worse. So even that was not the best option. If she didn't get the tube, she also wouldn't get the medication. So IV feeding would be useless.

My brother's wife, Amy, worked at the hospital as a pharmacist, so anything needing clarification were made clear, She explained that the Swallow Test indicated she couldn't swallow. That even ice chips would very easily be aspirated. She was wheeled back into the room, put back in the bed, and my father pulls the nurse outside and around the corner—and by then a friend arrived, this guy I didn't know—and my father asks the nurse the results of her test.

"Why don't you ask in front of mommy?" I say.

The nurse cuts him off and says, "She has a right to know, and I will not discuss this with you unless she's present."

I thanked her, and we walked back into the room. The nurse addressed my mother directly. She told her that the Swallow Test indicated she was unable to swallow, would aspirate anything she tried to eat, was at risk for choking, that the Parkinson's meds can only be given orally, had to be digested, so the only possibility was a PEG tube. And that was the only option.

So she asked, "Do you have a Living Will?"

And my father says, "No." At that point my father and my brother get into an argument about why there is no Living Will. I don't remember if it was me or my brother who asked him, "Did it never occur to you that this day would ever come?" My father was crying. Denial. This was no time to have an argument about why; the fact remained that they never discussed what she had wanted.

A long time ago, before she got sick—twenty years ago—my mother told me that if she ever got like my grandmother, unable to take care of herself, she "wanted to be shot." I had

Yahrzeit

to repeat this to the nurse, saying we had discussed this in the past, and she looks at my mother and says, "Is that true?"

And it's the last whole word I can remember my mother saying: "Yes."

And the nurse looked at me, and said, "That's very clear." And so she continued to ask her a few questions: "So that means you do not want a PEG tube?"

And again: "Yes."

"You understand that means no nutrition, no food?"

"Yes."

So I was standing behind the nurse at that point, so she could talk as close to my mother as possible, and my father asked what that means, and she said, "It means your wife does not want to be fed, and wants to allow this to take its natural course."

And I'm watching my mother, and I think it was at that point that she realized she was going to die, that all the days she had left could now be counted on the fingers of one hand, and that was it. I saw her realization that she was about to die. And she just started to cry.

And she just cried for quite a while. And people held her hand, and hugged her.

My brother kept saying to her, "It's going to be all right, it's going to be all right."

My father kept saying, "Don't worry, Sheil, don't worry Sheil."

I, on the other hand, went up to her, and said, "I don't know why they're telling you everything's going to be all right. You know and I know what the truth is. You'll be fine, but you won't be here. Everybody loves you. You did good. Rest." And I kissed her on the forehead. She stopped crying, and a few minutes later she closed her eyes and fell asleep.

My father had brought in a CD player, and he was playing Johnny Cash, Nat King Cole, John Denver. I think her hearing was perfect. No TV, just music the entire time. The nurse had left at some point to go get the social worker to have her come up and talk about her options. It was a small room. I guess there were four of us in the room, Amy would pop up from time to time, so five. And directly above her, not four feet above her head, a bank of fluorescent lights on the wall, and fluorescent lights on the ceiling above, and

Yahrzeit

bells were dinging and people calling on the loudspeaker. It was not at all a restful room. So the social worker comes up and we go down the hall to talk—my mother was still sleeping and we needed out of the room for a while. I had Sef come with us because I actually depend on her sometimes to have a clear head when I don't. The social worker wants to talk to us about hospice, which I think is a great idea, and the sooner the better. She couldn't stay at the hospice in the hospital, because you can only stay there for three days, and starving to death can take up to two weeks. My father keeps saying he can't afford hospice. The social workers keeps saying Medicare would take care of it. "My insurance won't take care it." "Medicare will take care of it completely," back and forth.

She told him of Hospice by the Sea, which I have heard over and over is the best care anyone could ever want. He wants to see it first. He think it's going to be dingy, old.

"Is it going to be worse than the room she's in now, with the fluorescent lights and the loudspeaker?" I ask.

"I don't know," he says. "Why don't we go see it tomorrow morning?" he asks.

And my daughter asks him, "Why don't you go see it *now*?"

"Well, everyone's tired, maybe we should rest, see it tomorrow morning."

My daughter insisted: "Why don't you think of her? Get her out of that room, get her somewhere comfortable?"

I ask the social worker: "Can we do it tonight?"

"Yes."

Father didn't know if he'll like it, didn't know if he could afford it. Don't remember my brother saying much, but he probably did.

I asked my father, "What are your choices? Look at your choices. She can't stay her more than three days. You cannot bring her home. This is her only choice. If you like it when you see it, if you don't like it when you see it, if it's a palace or a dungeon, this is your only choice. Why are you putting it off?"

I looked at the social worker and she said, "He's right, this is all you can do."

And so arrangements were made to bring her to Hospice by the Sea that evening. It was

Yahrzeit

a Friday evening. So he wants to go there first to see what it was like. I look at the social worker and said, "Let's get her ready to go, we'll get the papers signed, we'll go to Hospice by the Sea first and be there when she arrives." I ask my father if that works for him, and it does.

In moments here and there, my daughter keeps asking me, "What did he think was going to happen? What did he think his other choices were?" In the meantime, she had called in to take off work for the evening. She told them she thought she might have to take off the next day or two. She could not afford to do this, but she did it anyway.

So I went back into the room to see her, got the papers signed, and got ourselves over to Hospice by the Sea. And my father is starting to fret: "I can't do this, I can't let her starve, what am I going to do?"

We get there and the place is absolutely gorgeous. It's quiet, she has a large room, could have had a party in her room. This is the idea behind the design—everyone can come to be with the person who's dying. We open up the doors in front of the room, and everything is built around this garden with beautiful tropical foliage.

I know at some point we ate, don't remember when, don't remember what. My mother gets there around 11:00 at night, and they bring her in to the room. My father asks for a cot, and they bring him a rollaway bed so he can sleep right next to her, and he goes to find the nurse in charge. And he is beginning to panic. I don't want to say he's not rational, but he's walking around nearly hand-wringing: "I can't let her starve, I can't do this to her, I can't watch her starve, I can't starve her to death!" There wasn't much that we could do to calm him down. The nurse explained that she couldn't eat anything, and she also wouldn't be able to drink anything. You can go twenty-one days or longer without food, but you can't go that long without water, and they expected her go to within seven to ten days. I asked about IV fluids. She explained that she couldn't do that, because as you die, your body doesn't process fluids properly, and that means no fluids.

My father is crying, as you might expect; I'm not handling this well either, but I'm the

Yahrzeit

one who has to. When my maternal grandmother died, despite the fact that my father and she hated one another, he fell apart, and I had to handle everything. Despite the fact that my second child had just been born, and I was out of work, evicted, and had moved back to south Florida to look for work, instead I had to handle funeral arrangements. My family doesn't handle this death business very well.

We talk to the nurse, and we decided they would settle down for the night, go to sleep, and we would be back in the morning. Just before we leave my mother starts making noises like she's hungry. This just makes my father more upset. And none of us knows what to do; there is absolutely nothing we can do about it. My father is asking if there's some way we can feed her. The nurse tells him that they can try feeding her—if she wants. But the likelihood is that she will choke. And their recommendation is that would not be the best thing. Let her go to sleep, let her rest.

So I go back to my daughter's apartment with her and settle myself down on the couch, and it's too short for me, which is really saying something. It's about 1:00 in the morning, I think.

I'm not going to be able to sleep anyway, so I decide to talk to my mother, me on the couch in my daughter's apartment, my mother in her room in the hospice. About two weeks prior I had gotten a copy of *The Tibetan Book of the Dead*, and had started memorizing it. I had no reason to do this; I don't like memorizing things. And so I decided to recite the first paragraph to my mother, first as it was written, and then departing from it, paraphrasing:

> O nobly-born, that which is called death hath now come. Thou art departing from this world, but thou art not the only one; death cometh to all. Do not cling, in fondness and weakness, to this life. Even though thou clingest out of weakness, thou hast not the power to remain here.... Be not attached to this world.
>
> O nobly-born, what which is death has come to you. You are leaving this world. Do not hold on. Let go. Rest.

Yahrzeit

O nobly-born, death is coming to you.
You are leaving this world. Rest.

I kept saying it again and again and again to my mother. And then I said to her, "Please don't do this to Daddy. You know he can't handle this. He can't watch you starve to death. Please just rest, and don't do this to him."

At some point I fell asleep saying this. And then I hear a phone ring. It's my daughter's cell phone. And know what the call is. Sef comes out of the bedroom, walks over to me and says, "Dad, Grandma died."

And I said, "I know."

I was curious why my father called my daughter instead of me. He insists he called me, but Adam and Sef are nowhere close on his cellphone address list. It was five minutes before six. We got up, got dressed, not slowly but not quickly—we were both exhausted and feeling a little spacey.

Sef drove to Hospice by the Sea, we stopped on the way for coffee at a Dunkin Donuts, we needed something—protein, milk, something, because Lord knows when we'd be eating again. Five minutes later we were at the hospice. My brother was already there. My father was by my mother. He was standing over her saying, "I only left her for a half hour." He was beside himself—he had gone home for some clothes and some food.

And I saw my mother. And the first thing that occurred to me is that she looked like a dried fish. There was nothing there. Empty. Gone. My father kept stroking her forehead, kissing her forehead, telling her, "It's going to be all right, it's going to be all right, this is not how it was supposed to go, we were supposed to go together," on and on and on, telling her she was beautiful, telling her she would going to be all right. I imagine he was telling himself that, but I really don't think he believed it. We—my brother, daughter and I—went to speak to the nurse. She told us that she really didn't understand it. A few minutes after my father left, my mother started aspirating liquid, that her body had stopped processing fluids completely. The nurse said she couldn't suction out her mouth fast enough, and that her heart congested and she simply died. She kept suctioning out her mouth to

Yahrzeit

make her as comfortable as she could, and it took about fifteen minutes. She died about five minutes before my father got back. The nurse said she had never seen someone in this state go so quickly; it should have taken at least three days, minimum, probably five to seven. She really did not understand.

I told her I did.

And that was Saturday morning.

I know we had to get my father to eat; I'm not sure where we went or what we did. I think my brother took my father out while we waited with the body. My daughter and I waited because someone had to be there with the body until someone came to claim her, and that way we could give each other periodic breaks. Good thing we stopped to get her coffee; that had been my daughter's idea, and she's always right.

The funeral home arrived for the body around 9:30 in the morning, a very large man in a suit. I was supposed to make sure she was going to the right funeral home—my father was worried—so he could get the right dress to her; I was supposed to give the man a ring that he could put on her finger. So he's wrapping her up, in the shroud first, and up to this point I have not cried. As soon as he put the cloth over her face, that was it: I started crying. He puts her in the body bag, and wheels her out.

I went and thanked everyone at the hospice. They told me they were worried about my father, and wanted to make sure he was getting care. I said I rather doubted that he would. He had spent fifteen years taking care of her. There were times when we were not sure whether he was doing a good job or not, but how were we to know, and what could we do? We tried making him get respite care, but he said he couldn't afford it, yet he never checked with Medicare. We tried getting him support care for himself, but he wouldn't' do it. At the hospital we were told that my mother was in wonderful shape. They rarely see people at her stage so well taken care of, and the job he did taking care of her was, in the nurse's words, "heroic." But I seriously doubt that he'd get any care for himself at this point.

My daughter insists we go back to the apartment, shower, eat breakfast. She takes

Yahrzeit

me to Flakowitz of Boyton, a rather famous deli and restaurant. It's crowded, a Saturday morning, she says the place is good. I fret about not being able to find food that's good for me. She tells me, "Eat what you want, your mother just died!"

I said, "You mean, I can have comfort food?"

She tells me to shut up and get what I want. I don't remember what I got, but I remember it was really good.

As I eat, it dawns on me. I am a motherless child. I say this out loud. Sef nods. I say, "This will take some getting used to. I wonder how long."

"It's only been a few hours," she says. She wishes she knew her grandmother when she was able. She became sick when she was ten. She didn't know her when she hiked, rode bikes, prospected for precious stones played croquette, gardened, pained, did woodwork. When Sef knew her, she was barely still able to crochet.

My son does not know her without a wheelchair, barely able to speak.

I think we were meeting with the rabbi around 1 at the Funeral Home of Lantana, about 20 minutes north of there. It was Shabbos, which means my mother could not be buried that day. It's Jewish tradition to bury the dead within 24 hours unless it's Shabbos, in which case it's two days. At some point that morning I called my wife, Lee, and let her know. She had known my mother for about thirty years, so it was more than just her mother-in-law having died. She said she would throw some clothing in a bag for me, something appropriate for a funeral, and she would rent a car and come down, and she'd be there sometime that afternoon. We had only one car at that point.

We all met with the rabbi, and I instantly liked this fellow. He wanted us to write down things about my mother, things he should mention, things her friends would know, things he should know; he wanted us to treat him as though he would have been her friend. He made sure he pronounced her name properly, what she would want to be called, what she would want people to know. Then there was the matter of planning the funeral day. It was Saturday, the funeral would have to be Monday.

Yahrzeit

"Why not Sunday?" I asked.

"We can't get the grave dug by then."

"Why not?"

"We don't have gravediggers on Saturday. We'd have to pay them time-and-a-half."

In Jewish tradition, someone has to sit with the body continually until it is buried and say prayers over it, and that's a paid position, a *shomer*. We'd have to pay a shomer to sit for two days. I ask the rabbi how much that would be. He gave us the figure. I ask him how much time-and-a-half for gravediggers would be. There was a ten-dollar difference in cost, about $250 more one way or the other. So I suggested we simply ask the gravediggers to come in and work some overtime, and spare some old Jew who didn't know my mother from sitting with her and saying prayers over her. So that was settled.

We met my wife and my son Alek at the Ft. Lauderdale airport where the car had to be turned in, and we went to get a hotel room. I wanted an inexpensive hotel room; my wife wanted a nice one. We ended up at Embassy Suites. Why? "Because," my wife said. "Because your mother just died!"

That week my father-in law went into the hospital for a cardiac catheterization. I think that was it. But he was surprisingly blocked, especially considering the excellent care he takes of himself including his diet. He ended up in surgery and was, understandably unsettled. Lee needed to see him. It was bad timing, to be sure, but it was what it was. I could not stand to be by myself so I went to Pembroke Pines with my wife and kids to see my in-laws.

My mother-in law hugged me, asked if I was ok, did her best to be kind. I was exhausted and sat. My father-in-law wanted to talk and did so. He talked to me for nearly three hours straight. I dozed, woke, nodded, listened, dozed. He talked as though nothing different had happened to me today. As though today, for me, was nothing of note, was any other day.

We left. Lee commented on how good I was. I would normally have brushed the comment aside. Not this time. Yes. I was. Better than could be expected. Better than was reasonable. Above and beyond. Lee squeezed my hand and we headed back to Deerfield Beach.

Yahrzeit

That evening, we ate dinner—the whole family was together—and I watched how differently people handled the obviously empty space. There was an empty seat next to my father. I thought it needed to be empty for a while; my brother wanted me to move over and fill it. We sat there for a long time; I don't remember what we talked about.

I feel crooked. I feel unbalanced. Like one shoulder has a weight the other does not. Like one ear is sensing movement differently than the other. A part of me that has been around for 45 years, that my brain has developed knowing was there, is suddenly gone. It does not feel right. The world does not feel right. It is lopsided. I no longer have two parents. I have one. Something is missing. I wonder how long this will last.

Back to the hotel room. Lee drags me down to the pool and the hot tub. We walk on the beach for a while, then go to the hot tub. A blazered gentleman came over and said the hot tub is closed, it's past midnight. She tells him he really needs to sit in the hot tub tonight. He says, "But the rules say the hot tub closes at 11." She tells him my mother just died. He said, "Stay as long as you want." At some point she also got two gin and tonics down me, which is one-and-a-half more than I usually drink.

The funeral was set for 11. I had called my oldest friend, Carol, to let her know. She knows me since I'm 13 or 14; she insisted on coming to the funeral. I don't remember who else I called. The next morning I'm getting dressed. I pull out the pants and they are not mine. Apparently my wife brought a pair of her black pants, a drawstring number, pleated, which looked very nice—on *her*. It's Sunday morning; my father wears a size 42, so nothing he has will fit me; my brother is six feet tall, nothing of his will fit me. Lee's pants do fit. So I wear the cute little drawstring number. I pull out the shirt. It is a black silk shirt. I figure if I wear this shirt, I will melt off at least half a dozen pounds before the funeral is over. I go to put on the shoes. They are my seventeen-year-old son's skater shoes. But they fit me. So I am not quite dressed in the manner one would generally assume a son should dress for a funeral.

Yahrzeit

We headed to the funeral, which was held at the cemetery. We start at the chapel. This is the same cemetery where my father's mother is buried. The couples are buried one on top of each other. There are four spots, each for a couple, so it's a two-story underground concrete sealed horror. The caskets are lowered, then a concrete slab is lowered on top of that, then the marble lowered on top of that. Originally my father and my mother were supposed to be next to his mother and father, but my mother insisted she wanted to be at the other end of the grave "condos." Those who have read "Funeral, Expurgated" will understand why.

People start arriving. Some are crying, many are in wheelchairs. They were very involved in Americans with Disabilities Act activities. I don't remember a lot about the funeral except that I felt terribly self-conscious about what I was wearing. Carol found me and hugged me, and we went off and talked for a while, she and myself and Lee.

At some point my father went to the casket, and opened it up to look at her. He asked me if I wanted to. I said I didn't think I could.

Then we were told it was time to take our seats. My father, brother, and I were in the first row; Carol sat behind me; Lee, Sef, and Alek sat behind her. It was a bit of a wait, maybe five minutes, for the funeral to start. I leaned back and said to Carol, "These pants are chafing a bit, but I look so cute in them! Leave it to me to get into my wife's pants at my mother's funeral!" She starts laughing. A few other people laughed. A few people did not find it funny. I'm sure, however, that my mother would have, and I was fine with that.

Carol knew the rabbi, said he was a perfect choice, and indeed he was. He did a wonderful job, though I don't remember any of the details. You would think he had known her. He was splendid. The rabbi asked if anyone would like to speak. I raised my hand. Later my brother would tell me, "I knew you wouldn't be able to not speak," and I said, "I knew you wouldn't be able to, so I figured I would."

I told everyone that I had learned my sense of morals from her, and if that's all she'd ever taught me, it would have been enough. I said that the last thing I had told my mother was

Yahrzeit

that everyone loved her, that she did good, and that it was time to rest. I don't think I spoke for more than a minute. We moved out to the graveside. I immediately went to the casket to help roll it to the grave. "You don't have to," I was told. But of course I did. I literally buried my grandmother; I would certainly have done the same thing for my mother, if I could have. The least I could do was help push the casket out to the grave.

One of the four graveworkers stands aside so I can help roll the casket out. Even the grave workers are dressed better than I am. It's a long walk from the chapel to the grave, and it's August 30 in south Florida in a treeless cemetery. I am wearing a black silk shirt, black linen pants, black suede shoes, and it's a loooooong walk to the grave. I don't remember what was said at graveside; I know that *Kaddish* was said. I know that other prayers were said. There was a canopy with some chairs set for people; I stood by the grave the entire time.

And then the funeral was over. The casket was ready to be lowered into the grave, which is done by machine (this is *not* how most Jewish funeral go), and I had my hand on the casket as far down as I could—I'd have preferred lowering it ropes myself, but that wasn't available; I think we definitely lose something by having all this stuff mechanized. We were given little plastic baggies of dirt, about the size of two ketchup packets, to throw on to the casket. I wanted a shovel and a pile of dirt, and what I got were tiny baggies. I wanted to bury her and all I could throw in was a teaspoon of dirt, so I grabbed all that I could find—it didn't matter if anyone else had any.

We were then told that it was time to leave, because it was time to bring in the backhoe to load in the concrete that would be lowered halfway down the condo so it would be covering my mother's casket. The canopy had to go. The plywood on which the seats sat had to be moved so the backhoe wouldn't eat up the grass.

And I told them: "No." Very matter of fact. No. I was going to help, until it was completely sealed. I told the rabbi, "I don't get a shovel, I don't get any dirt, but I'm going to damn well see this thing sealed." He said he understood.

Yahrzeit

The first piece of concrete had a bolt hole in each corner. Large eyes were screwed into each, chains attached to those, the four chains attached to a hook on the backhoe. It was picked up moved, positioned, lowered. And I stood there, a little too close for safety, until I could catch the last glimpse of the coffin as the slab covered it. Then one of the workers had to jump in and unscrew the bolts and take the chains off. Lee wisely kept me from doing that; I was very bothered by someone I didn't know jumping into my mother's grave, silly me.

Then came the second concrete slab to cover the top half of the two-story grave. Same process. I helped unscrew the bolts and take off the chains, since this was just below ground level and I could reach it. Then the same process for the marble grave top. It's positioned into place with my hand on it. I helped take off the chains, unscrew the eyes. And then the workers come over with a bolt and a large brass washer, and that is screwed on, attaching it to the concrete grave box.

I said to one of the workers, "Mind if I do that?"

And he says, "You're not supposed to."

And I said to him, an older black fellow, "If this was your mom, and you had no shovel and no dirt, what would you do?"

He said, "I would hand you the bolts and hand you the wrench and say, 'There you go.'" And he did. And I screwed my mother's grave closed.

That afternoon we—family, extended family, friends—went back to my brother's house. Amy had gone ahead, picked up platters of sandwiches and desserts. And we talked. I changed into normal clothes that were actually mine. I met the son of my mother's oldest friend. My father's brother came down. I sat with Amy and said that I would prefer that we manage to get together under circumstances other than this from time to time, that it would be nice. We were there about two hours before we left. Everyone needed rest. Lee and I and the kids headed to Carol's house. She had made us macaroni and cheese, and other assorted things we shouldn't eat, and we sat and talked. I needed that comfort after this weekend. Next to Lee, she's the person I've known the longest. Sometime around

Yahrzeit

six we left and drove home, less than a two-hour drive. I drove there with a mother. I drive home without one.

What Do Jews Do on Christmas?

What do Jews do on Christmas? Well
in the United States,
at least,
we take walks,
move,
find a park
We go out to the few open businesses,
movies theater, Chinese food,
and know that most everyone we see
   will be Jewish
or atheist (though they may still follow
   comfortable family tradition)
or what have you, but not Christian.
Here, the temperature is in the 70s
and we had a beautiful solstice under
   the stars
(we could see though the city-glow)

in our shirtsleeves
and on the 25th
we are at my sister-in-law's
(mother-in law, father-in-law, wife,
   daughter, and son)
because she doesn't want to be the only
   Jew at her home
as she gathers her husband's family—
Southern Baptists all
and very concerned for the souls of the
   children.
We are there with my mother-in-law
who was born Jewish
but who is sure America has made
   Christmas
a national holiday
we have to celebrate
or incur a terrible social wrath.
She wants to know if we are going to
   heaven.
(How the hell should I know?)
(Is it full of people just like this?)
Then the party is over,
everyone wishes each other Merry
   Christmas

What Do Jews Do on Christmas?

over piles of presents given each other
in honor of the Christ child
and we gave one or two but look at all
   that stuff! And say goodbye.

About the Author

ADAM **B**YRN **T**RITT, MEd, CH, LMT, is an internationally bestselling author, poet, essayist, screenwriter, teacher, social activist, and humorist. In 2012 his hilarious children's book, *Bud the Spud*, was published by Axios Press. In addition to *Yom Kippur as Manifest in an Approaching Dorsal Fin*, Tritt is the author of *Songs from the Well: A Memoir of Love*, the chronicle of his love for his wife, her sudden and heartbreaking loss to brain cancer, and his struggle to find a way back to life; *The Phoenix and the Dragon: Poems of the Alchemical Transformation*, a collection of his poetry; as well as several works of nonfiction including the bestselling *Tellstones: Runic Divination in the Welsh Tradition*.

Adam won the 2006 EPPIE Award for Poetry in an Anthology. In 1995 he was awarded an honorary doctorate for his work in religious tolerance and for the creation of TurningPoint, a nonprofit program providing alternative medicine to low-income individuals. He continues that passion today in the healthcare clinic he and his wife, Lee, dreamed of and created together—the Wellness Center.

He is equally at home speaking in lecture halls, giving public readings in bookstores, and visiting elementary school classrooms, where he can be found surrounded by children begging him to read *Bud the Spud* just one more time (while their parents and teachers beg him to stop).

Adam lives and writes—often simultaneously—in Palm Bay, Florida, with his son, daughter-in-law, and granddaughter; a dingo;

About the Author

and a ridiculously large alligator, all under a very big tree. His website is AdamTritt.com.

www.ingramcontent.com/pod-product-compliance
Lightning Source LLC
Chambersburg PA
CBHW052048070526
44584CB00017B/2099